Social Skills
Games
for Children

by the same author

Self-Esteem Games for Children
Deborah M. Plummer
Illustrated by Jane Serrurier
978 1 84310 424 7

Anger Management Games for Children
Deborah M. Plummer
Illustrated by Jane Serrurier
978 1 84310 628 9

Helping Children to Build Self-Esteem
A Photocopiable Activities Book
Second edition
Deborah M. Plummer
Illustrated by Alice Harper
978 1 84310 488 9

Helping Adolescents and Adults to Build Self-Esteem
A Photocopiable Resource Book
Deborah M. Plummer
978 1 84310 185 7

The Adventures of the Little Tin Tortoise
A Self-Esteem Story with Activities for Teachers, Parents and Carers
Deborah M. Plummer
978 1 84310 406 3

Using Interactive Imagework with Children
Walking on the Magic Mountain
Deborah M. Plummer
978 1 85302 671 3

Social Skills
Games
for Children

Deborah M. Plummer

Illustrated by Jane Serrurier

Foreword by Professor Jannet Wright

Jessica Kingsley Publishers
London and Philadelphia

First published in 2008
by Jessica Kingsley Publishers
116 Pentonville Road
London N1 9JB, UK
and
400 Market Street, Suite 400
Philadelphia, PA 19106, USA

www.jkp.com

Library of Congress Cataloging in Publication Data

Plummer, Deborah.
  Social skills games for children / Deborah M. Plummer ; foreword, Jannet Wright.
     p. cm.
  Includes bibliographical references and indexes.
  ISBN 978-1-84310-617-3 (pb : alk. paper) 1. Social skills in children--Study and teaching. 2. Interpersonal relations in children--Study and teaching. 3. Social interaction in children--Study and teaching. I. Title.
  HQ783.H59 2008
  372.82--dc22

British Library Cataloguing in Publication Data
A CIP catalogue record for this book is available from the British Library

ISBN 978 1 84310 617 3

Printed and bound in Great Britain by
Athenaeum Press, Gateshead, Tyne and Wear

Contents

List of games

Foreword

It is with great pleasure that I write this foreword for *Social Skills Games for Children*. This book will provide practitioners with new ideas for working in the area of social skills as well as giving experienced people suggestions for refreshing their repertoire of activities.

Deborah Plummer's book provides that rare combination – theoretical information and suggestions about how to put this information into practice. The games described in the book can be used by practitioners who are working with children of any age who need help in developing and using appropriate social skills. Some people will use the games to help children who struggle with this area of development, but all the activities described in this book can be used with any children to help them build on their existing skills and increase for example, their self-awareness, self-control and abilities in effective listening.

Practitioners working in educational settings in England will be particularly pleased to see how well the games link with individual behaviour plans and the content of the book as a whole fits well with The Children's Plan (2007). The activities described here can be used in a variety of settings including youth groups, play schemes, activity holidays as well as at home.

Social Skills Games for Children is the third book in a collection of games books written by Deborah, the other two books *Anger Management Games for Children* and *Self-Esteem Games for Children* also provide suggestions and activities which can be used with young children.

Deborah Plummer brings great expertise to the area of social skills. She qualified as a speech and language therapist which is when I first met her and she then went on to gain considerable experience in facilitating groups and working with children. Deborah now runs workshops and courses related to self-esteem. Throughout this book her theoretical knowledge, practical experience and desire to help children is evident. I recommend it to all those who are working with children.

Professor Jannet A. Wright
Head of the Speech and Language Therapy Division,
De Montfort University

Part One

Theoretical
and practical background

Introduction

Social Skills Games for Children offers ways to support children who are struggling to develop or to demonstrate their social skills and shows how youngsters can build on their existing skills for social interaction through the medium of games.

The underlying philosophy governing the use of games as a basis for learning comes from my experiences as a speech and language therapist and a deep belief that children have an amazing array of abilities which often go untapped in our rush to teach them what we know about life from an adult perspective. Play is a natural childhood activity and a child's imagination is a valuable inner resource which can be used to foster creative thinking, healthy self-esteem and the ability to interact successfully with others. Games that are facilitated mindfully and with integrity can provide a rich learning experience that goes beyond the teaching of skills as a way of masking or compensating for social ineptness and opens up the possibility of a much deeper learning instead – the type of learning that leads to socially intelligent interactions and promotes feelings of personal fulfilment and self-respect.

Why use non-competitive games?

This book is one of a collection based on the use of games to enhance social and emotional well-being (see *Self-Esteem Games for Children* and *Anger Management Games for Children*, also published by Jessica Kingsley Publishers). In line with the other books, *Social Skills Games for Children* also focuses on non-competitive games where the enjoyment and the challenge come from the process itself rather than from winning. This is not because I have an aversion to competitive games. In fact, I believe that these can form an important part of a child's learning once she is ready to engage in them and does so by her own choice. The child's world is after all a competitive arena and most children will naturally play games of skill that involve winning or losing or being 'in' or 'out' whether we adults encourage them or not. However, the ability to cope successfully in competition with peers is a tricky hurdle to negotiate and one which will complicate the process of focusing on the building of other social skills. Younger children and those who are particularly vulnerable to low self-esteem often find win or lose games extremely difficult to manage. For such children, the anticipation of the 'rewards' of winning might be so great that the disappointment of losing has an equally dramatic effect on their mood. In order to enjoy and benefit from competitive games they will therefore need to first develop a certain degree of emotional resilience, competence and self-efficacy, all of which can be fostered initially through non-competitive activities.

Who will benefit from social skills games?

The games are suitable for all children from 5 to 12 years of age. In the school setting they will fit into a wide selection of personal, social and health education (PSHE) and other learning objectives. They can be used to teach and enhance a variety of skills at primary level and to reinforce strategies for social interaction during the vulnerable period of transition to secondary education. The material can be incorporated into individual behaviour plans (IBPs) and can be used to target specific aspects of individual education plans (IEPs). The concepts fit with the ethos of The Children's Plan (DCSF 2007), an important element of the Government's Every Child Matters programme which sets out goals that include the participation of all children and young people in 'positive activities to develop personal and social skills' and which will include a specific play strategy to be published in 2008.

The games in this book can also be used to complement other approaches to social and emotional development currently promoted within the primary education system such as the SEAL programme (Social and emotional aspects of learning, DfES 2005).[1]

Children attending after school clubs, youth groups and play schemes will enjoy and benefit from engaging in the activities and crucially, all the games can be played at home by families. The central role played by parents and carers (and often by the wider family network) in supporting a child's social and emotional development is of course tremendously important. The special time shared during a fun game can be a boost to helping family members to understand each other, show their love, and strengthen their relationship. Sharing moments of laughter, problem-solving and creativity during games can be rewarding and re-affirming for everyone concerned.

The material will also complement intervention methods used in a diverse range of therapy approaches with individual children or groups, including existing social skills programmes.

---

1   The DfES (Department for Education and Skills) ceased to exist in June 2007 and was replaced by the DCSF (Department for Children, Schools and Families).

Strategies are outlined for helping children to transfer skills to a variety of different situations and to maintain their progress, particularly at times of stress, and facilitators are invited to reflect on their own interactions with children and to consider how this reflection can support the process of change.

How the games are structured

The games and activities are divided into nine sections, including warm-ups and wind-downs. This division is designed to aid the process of evaluating and adapting games to suit specific needs. In practice, many of the games could be placed in more than one section and you will find that you are often touching on several aspects of social skills within just one game.

Each game has been marked with a set of symbols to aid in the selection of the most appropriate ones for different groups of children:

⑤	This gives an indication of the suggested *youngest* age for playing the game. There is no upper age limit given.
⏲ 10 mins	An approximate time is suggested for the length of the game (excluding the discussion time). This will obviously vary according to the size of the group and the ability of the players.
♦ ♦ ♦	Indicates that the game is suitable for larger groups (eight or more).
♦ ♦	The game is suitable for small groups.
♀♀♀	The game involves a lot of speaking unless it is adapted.
♀♀	A moderate amount of speaking is required by players.
♀	The game is primarily a non-verbal game or one requiring minimal speech.
☑ empathy	This gives an indication of a foundation ability or specific skill used or developed by playing this game.

Foundation abilities and specific skills

There is an inherent difficulty involved in compiling a definitive list of social skills since each of our social interactions is of course unique and dependent on such aspects as who is involved (taking account of culture, gender, age and developmental factors); what has brought them together; the goal of the interaction; the environment; and the mood and previous experiences of each participant.

However, there are certain recognizable core abilities which underpin the socially intelligent selection and use of appropriate behaviours. Each of these abilities is specifically addressed by different sets of games in Part Two. They are:

- Self-awareness – a child's ability to be aware of her feelings, thoughts and behaviour and also of her own needs in social interactions (Chapter 9: Staying on track).

- Self-control – her belief that she has some control over her feelings and thoughts and the ways in which she expresses them; an ability to manage impulsivity and to show emotions appropriately (Chapter 9: Staying on track).

- Effective listening – her ability to really hear what others are saying and to reflect on what she hears. This involves attention control and is an important pre-requisite for being able to negotiate and cooperate (Chapter 10: Tuning in).

- Effective observation – her ability to observe and reflect on non-verbal aspects of interactions such as changes in facial expression and body posture (Chapter 10: Tuning in).

- The ability to understand and use verbal and/or non-verbal forms of communication with others (Chapter 11: More than just talking).

- A knowledge and understanding of a range of different emotions and how to cope with other people's emotions. For example, noticing when someone is upset and offering to help (Chapter 12: You and me).

- Imagination – an important element of empathy: her ability to see things from another person's point of view and to be aware of other people's needs (Chapter 12: You and me).

- Tolerance and respect of differences and knowing how to convey this (Chapter 13: You and me together).

- The ability to understand the 'mutuality' involved in cooperation and negotiation (Chapter 13: You and me together).

- The ability to apply appropriate problem-solving strategies (Chapter 14: Got it!).

Within this framework for social competence there are certain *behaviours* which demonstrate the abilities. For example, in relation to being able to cooperate and negotiate successfully in a verbal exchange any or all of the following communication skills may be utilized:

- initiating and ending an interaction
- asking/answering questions

- making requests
- taking turns in conversation
- giving personal information
- explaining/giving instructions
- encouraging and reinforcing others
- giving and receiving specific praise
- keeping an interaction going/staying on the subject
- flexibility in communication style
- being appropriate and timely in interactions
- awareness of appropriate personal space (proximity to others).

The lists of skills and foundation abilities provided for each game have been limited to just a few key areas but you may find that you want to add others relevant to your own focus of work. Undoubtedly, the more often that you play these games, the more you will want to add to each list.

Adaptations

Ideas for expanding and adapting the games are offered as a starting point for your own experimentation with the main themes. Most games can be adapted appropriately to enable children with diverse strengths and needs to take part. Older children should also be given plenty of opportunities to invent new versions of familiar games and to alter the rules of games in discussion with other group members. Experimentation with the structure of games helps children to understand the value of rules and to distinguish more easily between what works and what doesn't. Discussion with peers also provides opportunities for developing skills in negotiating and decision making. Before any alterations are made it is of course important to make it clear to all players that there are certain safety and non-discriminatory rules which must always be followed.

Reflections and notes

Personal reflection and reflections about the games themselves are a vital part of the learning process – even the briefest time spent in thinking about behaviour and feelings or actions and consequences can help children to make enormous leaps in realization.

Valuing children's views about a games session is also likely to foster increased motivation to engage more fully in the learning process, and their comments about a particular game could guide you in choosing another game to address that specific issue.

Suggestions for discussion with older children are provided after each game description. As a general principle I would suggest that we should not give more time to a discussion at the time of playing than we do to the game itself. Many children who play games regularly eventually gain insights into their own behaviour and emotions and those of others purely through the experience, and will not necessarily need to take specific time to reflect on what happened within every session. However, these topics do also provide an opportunity for drawing links between different themes at later times. You could remind children of particular games when this is relevant: 'Do you remember when we played that game of...' 'What did you feel when...?' or 'How might this game help us to understand what happened in the class yesterday?'

The suggestions for discussion can also provide focus points for you to use during your own planning and reflection sessions (see pp.51–3 for further guidelines). To aid this process, each game description includes space for you to add your own notes. These might include such things as personal insights and experiences of using the games, personal preferences, dislikes, problems and successes, and any issues raised concerning age, cultural or gender differences etc.

Additional notes

Finally, because you will undoubtedly have many more games in your repertoire and will gather extra ideas from colleagues and children, each of the games sections ends with a blank summary page for 'additional notes'. Here you can add to your list and make any further general comments on your experiences with the games that you have used.

My hope is that this format will encourage reflective practice but that it will not discourage enjoying the pure fun of playing games with young children. This, after all, is one of the essential values of this approach – having fun while learning about ourselves and others!

Integrating games into different settings

The ways in which the games are adapted and incorporated into family life and into educational and therapy approaches can and should vary according to the setting and according to the needs, strengths and experiences of the children. Each adult who facilitates games will naturally bring his or her own personality, imagination, expertise and knowledge to the games and create something new from the basic format. Also, because of the nature of group dynamics, the same game played with a different group will inevitably have a different feel to it and probably have different outcomes for the participants. In this way, playing with the process of playing becomes an integral part of our own learning.

However, the games in this book do follow a logical progression. If you are structuring sessions based specifically around the development of social skills, I suggest that you always start with a warm-up game (Chapter 8: Getting to know each other), followed by two or three games from one of the subsequent sections (or from two consecutive sections), and finish with a relaxation/wind-down game.

Warm-ups and ice-breakers foster group cohesion and help to develop a group identity. They encourage children to interact with each other, and help them to feel that they have been acknowledged by everyone else. They act as a ritual to mark the beginning of a session and to ensure that each person has fully 'arrived' in the group.

The relaxations and wind-downs emphasize the skills involved in managing levels of emotion and teach simple strategies for 'letting go' of any left over feelings which may have arisen during earlier games and discussions, or which may occur in the future. This combination is important because children need to feel safe and contained when they are exploring social and emotional skills. The structure of a games session can facilitate this by providing predictability and certainty.

The focus of each game should be made explicit where appropriate. For example, you might introduce a warm-up game by telling the children that it is a game for getting to know each other better. Where you are intending to follow a game with a discussion about a specific social skill you might set the focus with a more detailed introduction, perhaps by telling a short story or recounting a fictitious event to illustrate a particular use or misuse of a social skill. You could then introduce the chosen game(s) as being a way of exploring that skill. On completion of the game(s) 'debrief' or discuss what happened during play. As children become used to the format they can be encouraged to choose familiar games (perhaps from a small selection of possible options) which they think might be relevant for a particular skill. This process of choosing can also engender useful discussions about how skills are learned and developed.

Further guidelines for facilitating the games can be found in Chapter 4: Structuring the emotional environment.

Understanding social skills[1]

Key concepts

- The foundations for social skills are laid down in infancy.

- A child's ability to engage in socially skilled interactions is also related to the successful development of a range of cognitive processes.

- Naturally occurring periods of heightened self-awareness may result in vulnerable children becoming more isolated.

- Social skills difficulties can be specific or more generalized.

- Children who fail to develop appropriate social skills often continue to experience problems in later life.

- Helping children to build social skills will enable them to develop a balance between the formation of healthy relationships and personal autonomy.

Four-year-old Jack is playing with his favourite toy animals in an Early Years classroom. He has constructed an elaborate farm yard on the floor and is busy loading sheep into a plastic truck. When Alex sits down next to him Jack pushes him away forcefully, saying 'You can't play!' Alex

---

1 For an outline of the social skills covered by the games in Part Two please see *Foundation abilities and specific skills*, pp.15–17.

begins to cry. Four-year-old Hannah, who is evidently disturbed by her classmate's tears, watches from a distance for a few moments and then silently offers Alex the doll that she has been playing with. When this doesn't console him she briefly puts her arm around him and then goes to fetch one of the adults.

Hannah is demonstrating two very crucial aspects of social competence: she is making a connection with the emotions of another child and she is attempting to repair the situation by trying out a range of learnt strategies. She is discovering that handling another person's emotions is no easy task and that sometimes adult intervention might be the best option!

Like most children, it seems that Hannah is learning social skills by observing others and through a process of trial and error. When something works well for her it is likely to be reinforced in some way, for example by verbal praise from an adult, by resolution of a difficult situation or by her own internal sense of calm. Successful interactions will tend to have a positive effect on others and are likely to lead to increased social contact and more opportunities for Hannah to alter and refine her skills. Eventually, she will be able to call on different sets of appropriate behaviour for different situations, utilizing what is often referred to as 'social intelligence'.

But what if we were to discover that Hannah's mother suffers from bouts of depression and is often unresponsive to Hannah's emotional needs? In fact, Hannah is ambivalent and insecure in her relationship with her mother and, in consequence, has become hyper-sensitive to other people's mood changes. Or what if we learn that Jack has autism and cannot tolerate interference in his game, or that Alex and his twin brother are in separate classes for the first time today? Now this seemingly simple interaction suddenly reveals itself as being more complex and more poignant as each child tentatively engages in the social 'dance' that reflects his or her early life experiences.

The foundations for social skills are laid down in infancy

The early interaction patterns between babies and their care-givers play a crucial part in the development of social skills, both in terms of particular behaviours and, as we now know, in the chemical and neurological make-up of the baby's brain. When parents are sensitive and responsive to their child's needs and moods they naturally engage in interactions which reinforce such skills as turn-taking, eye gaze, interpreting and mirroring facial expressions and the ability to initiate enjoyable interactions. Sensitive parenting also encourages the establishment of an effective emotion-regulation system: the baby's ability to self-regulate and self-calm so that he or she is not constantly overwhelmed with difficult emotions. Parents who are attuned to their baby's feelings will automatically provide the comfort and touch which allows the emotion-regulation system to develop and to function effectively. But research shows that where this natural process is inhibited there may be long-term consequences:

> Stress in infancy – such as consistently being ignored when you cry – is particularly hazardous because high levels of cortisol in the early months of life can also affect the development of other neurotransmitter systems whose pathways are still being established… When stressed, these various biochemical systems may become skewed in ways that make it more difficult for the individual to regulate himself in later life. (Gerhardt 2004, p.65)

These early experiences affect the development of the pre-frontal cortex – the area of the brain that deals with feelings and with social interactions. The pre-frontal cortex plays a vital role in inhibiting or regulating the more primitive responses of the amygdala – the area of the brain which deals with the fear and self-defence systems – and is most vulnerable to outside influences during its critical period of development in the first four years of life.

Without a well-developed pre-frontal cortex children will not only have difficulty with self-control and self-regulation but also with the ability to feel 'connected' to others. It has been found that some four-year-olds who have been brought up in chaotic and stressful environments (for example where there has been severe neglect or abuse) have a measurably smaller pre-frontal cortex compared to four-year-olds who have experienced a nurturing environment. These children show clear signs of lack of social competence, an inability to manage stress and the inability to see things from another child's viewpoint (Gerhardt 2004).

Where development has been unimpeded however, even very young children are capable of showing 'prosocial and reparative behaviours such as helping, sharing, sympathizing, and comforting victims' (Harter 1999, p.111).

Although negative experiences may make it extremely difficult for a child to empathize with others and to understand social signals, there is fortunately much that can be done to redress the damage. The brain is remarkable in its capacity to adapt and respond to new influences, particularly during early childhood. Supportive interactions and the teaching of key skills can therefore greatly enhance a child's capacity for self-control, self-regulation and connection to others.

A child's ability to engage in socially skilled interactions is related to the successful development of a range of cognitive processes

With increasing maturity, a child's thought processes and the ways in which she appraises situations will start to play a bigger part in how she interprets social interactions and in how she monitors and evaluates her own skills. There is a strong link, for example, between social understanding (learning about how other people think, feel and behave) and social skills. In particular, a great deal of research has focused on children's ability to understand that people can misrepresent true facts and events but will nevertheless still base their behaviour on these misrepresentations or 'false beliefs'. This understanding of false beliefs appears to emerge some time between four and six years of age and has been linked with such social skills as the ability to play cooperatively and to follow rules in simple games (Lalonde and Chandler 1995 cited in Carpendale and Lewis 2006).

By seven or eight years of age (coinciding with the point of entry into the next stage of education and the changes associated with this) most children will have developed an ability to make judgements about different interpretations of events and will be more able to understand and tolerate ambiguity. This will help them to be accepting of others and to make more informed judgements about appropriate behaviour.

Naturally occurring periods of heightened self-awareness may result in vulnerable children becoming more isolated

It is also around the age of seven that children become much more self-aware and begin to compare themselves more directly with their peers. A child who has healthy self-esteem and age-appropriate social skills will usually weather this period well, striking a healthy balance between forming friendship groups and learning to be self-reliant. However, when children do not have this solid foundation, an increase in self-awareness may lead to feelings of acute vulnerability in terms of being 'judged' by others. This can be particularly noticeable with some children who have a communication or learning difficulty. Whereas such children may have appeared to cope well during their early years it is at this point that they may begin to withdraw from social contact or from participation in group activities. Social anxiety and negative expectations of how others will view them is also likely to have a direct influence on how children communicate when they do engage in interactions resulting in further misunderstandings, embarrassment and confirmation of their difficulties.

The period of transition to secondary school is another common point at which children may experience heightened social anxiety and awareness of moments of social ineptness. Popularity with peers becomes an increasingly important issue for this age group at a time when they are also trying to cope with the challenges of larger groups and of taking more responsibility for themselves and for their learning. A child who already has difficulties with understanding and using appropriate social skills will undoubtedly find this transition period even more confusing and overwhelming. This could result in withdrawal or in further development of inappropriate behaviour in an attempt to gain recognition from peers.

It is an unfortunate truth that while someone who has a physical problem in coordinating muscle movements may be seen by their peers as clumsy but 'doing their best', someone who is *socially* clumsy is much more likely to be seen as 'odd' or not fitting in with the social norm – a difficult and painful situation which can all too often lead to rejection or ridicule from others.

Social skills difficulties can be specific or more generalized

Child psychologists Stephen Nowicki and Marshall Duke, have used the term *dyssemia* to describe the very specific difficulty that some children have with understanding and using non-verbal communication. They believe that because children are not specifically taught about non-verbal aspects of communication (except through observation of others) many fail to learn some of the basic 'non-verbal rules'. In their book *Helping the Child Who Doesn't Fit In* they describe typically dyssemic children as those who 'may stand too close to others, touch them inappropriately, or misunderstand and misinterpret friendly actions.' (Nowicki and Duke 1992, p.5).

As already mentioned, sometimes the difficulty is not due to a failure to learn a specific skill but is the byproduct of a more general learning or communication difference:

Meera is ten. She has a hearing impairment and her language development is delayed. She has found it difficult to learn the social rules that will help her to interact successfully with her peers. Waiting her turn in a group activity is proving very difficult for her. She fidgets and calls out while other children are having their turn.

Theo is nine. He has Asperger syndrome and is struggling to join in with the classroom discussion about bullying. He is becoming increasingly anxious and is particularly agitated by the fact that some of the other children are sitting in close proximity to him.

Françoise is 12. She is dyslexic and has problems with organizational skills and short-term memory. She did not remember that she was supposed to meet her friend at the bus stop today. Now her friend has sent her an angry text. Françoise is upset but is unsure how to respond.

Social competence is a 'dance' between all participants – with each person appraising and adjusting the nuances of interaction, often at a subconscious level. It is hardly surprising that many children struggle to join the dance, or that they dance to a different tune, or with different steps.

Children who fail to develop appropriate social skills often continue to experience problems in later life

Whatever the causal factors, the consequences of social ineptness can be far-reaching. Children who do not learn to master the social dance are often seen as insensitive or big-headed and may be quick to anger because they misread social signals. Their awkwardness and anxiety may cause others around them to feel anxious in their presence and their consequent negative social experiences may lead to chronic low self-esteem and interfere with their learning. Various studies have also demonstrated a link between childhood difficulties with social interaction and later problems in adulthood, such as persistent anxiety and depression. In extreme cases, inappropriate social interactions can lead to complete social rejection. As Daniel Goleman points out, people who fail to follow the unspoken rules of social harmony 'inevitably leave disturbance in their wake' (Goleman 1996, p.121).

Helping children to build social skills will enable them to develop a balance between the formation of healthy relationships and personal autonomy
Clearly, it is important to help all children to negotiate social situations, connect with others and form appropriate friendships in ways that are suitable for their current developmental level and learning abilities. At the same time, we should also take into account the need to foster healthy self-esteem, self-reliance and self-respect. This balance between healthy connectedness with others and personal autonomy is described by developmental psychologist Susan Harter as 'mutuality'. Harter stresses that this is qualitatively different to a simple combination of the two – it is more of an active balance of 'much less extreme forms' (Harter 1999, p.295).

Allied to these principles is the notion of self-efficacy – the belief that we are capable of doing something and that we can influence events that affect our lives (for example, Bandura 1977). A sense of self-efficacy allows individuals to make intelligent use of social skills to influence others. This adds important ethical and moral aspects to the interpretation of social competence. We probably all know of someone who is skilled enough in social intercourse to be able to manipulate others for their own objectives. Where interactions occur in the spirit of mutuality however, then outcomes are likely to be beneficial to everyone concerned.

I firmly believe that when we help children to develop their social skills we are doing much more than just helping them to fit in with those around them. We are giving them the tools for social intelligence and personal fulfilment – we are promoting mutual respect and understanding whilst still recognizing and celebrating the integrity of the individual.

Cooperative games provide an ideal vehicle for such learning. They can easily be adapted in order to revisit different skills at later stages, thus expanding each child's repertoire of appropriate behaviours and giving him more choice and flexibility in how he initiates and participates in social interactions. Some of the many learning opportunities provided by playing games are explored in the next chapter.

Why use games to support social skills?

Key concepts

- Play is a serious business!
- Learning through play is a natural part of a child's development.
- Games:

  ◦ provide structure and predictability

  ◦ reflect aspects of real life

  ◦ provide valuable learning opportunities.

Play is a serious business!

Why is it that some games seem to 'work' well with one group and not with another? I believe that one of the main reasons lies in how well the person who is facilitating the games understands the importance of the game process and how powerful this process can be. Of course, games played as energizers or treats can be exciting and fun and a source of immense pleasure for the players. Occasionally, however, they can also be sheer torture for the quiet child, the child who has difficulty understanding the rules of games, the child who is already full of pent up frustration or anxiety, or who fears being 'left out' or losing yet again. In these circumstances some games may heighten feelings of low self-esteem in children and trigger uncomfortably intense or inappropriate emotional responses.

In contrast, a well-chosen game played with awareness on the part of the facilitator can be an incredibly effective instrument for supporting a child's emergent sense of self and for helping him to tolerate frustration and learn to cooperate with his peers.

Games provide a fun way of learning serious ideas and important life skills. When they are facilitated by adults they should always be played mindfully and with integrity. We need to be fully aware of why we are playing the games that we have chosen; fully conscious of the possible effects that playing such games might have; and fully 'present' with the children in order to understand their ways of responding and interacting and to appreciate the spontaneous learning that is occurring within and between group members.

Learning through play is a natural part of a child's development

The universality of play and traditional games highlights the developmental importance of this aspect of children's learning. From early babyhood, through our childhood years and often into adulthood (through sports activities for example) play is how we find out about ourselves and the world. This process begins through manipulation of our own body (e.g. sucking a thumb or toes); play with sounds (babbling); play with objects (e.g. a comfort blanket or a soft toy) and play with significant people in our lives (e.g. the 'mirroring' of facial expression and body movements that often occurs so naturally between a parent and child, games of peek-a-boo and waving 'bye bye'). In this way we gradually learn what is 'me' and 'not me', we learn the rudiments of cause and effect and turn-taking. We even learn to cope with feelings of temporary separation and loss with games such as hide-and-seek and peek-a-boo.

From this type of play we move on gradually to symbolic play – manipulation of objects as symbols of real things – and then to imaginary play where some props may be used but much, or all, of the scenario is imagined. This type of engagement in the world of imagination gradually moves from solitary or parallel play to engagement in play with others: 'I'm the Mummy and I have to feed the baby,' 'I will be the princess and you can be the wicked witch' or 'I'm a policeman and I'm looking for a robber.'

By working our imagination like a muscle we learn to problem-solve, to tolerate frustration, to work through some of life's difficulties and so reach our own 'child-level' of understanding of the complexities of the world – we make 'child-sense' of our experiences in a simplified and safe way and thereby strengthen our emotional resilience.

Play of one sort or another provides invaluable opportunities for children to learn through imitation, to experience the consequences of their actions and to experiment with different skills and different outcomes without fear of failure or being judged unfavourably by others. It is also through play that children can expand and consolidate their language skills.

Psychologist Catherine Garvey suggests that:

> because playing is voluntarily controlled (executed in a way in which imperfect achievement is minimally dangerous), its effects are probably intricately related to the child's mastery and integration of his experiences…when the behaviour is next performed in a non-play mode, it may be more skilled, better integrated, and associated with a richer or wider range of meaning. In this way play can contribute to the expertise of the player and to his effectiveness in the non-play world. (Garvey 1977, p.118)

Vivian Paley has also documented many crucial observations of the importance of children's play. As a nursery teacher she became increasingly aware of how children in her classes placed a great deal of emphasis on things that happened during play activities – it was the themes that arose during play that they were most likely to want to discuss. In her wonderful book *The Boy Who Would Be a Helicopter* Paley observes that children's rites and images in play:

> seem mainly concerned with the uses of friendship and fantasy to avoid fear and loneliness and to establish a comfortable relationship with people and events. In play, the child says, 'I can *do* this well; I can *be* this effectively; I *understand* what is happening to me and to other children.' (Paley 1991, p.10)

As with all areas of emotional and social development, we now know that pleasurable, playful experiences affect the chemical balance and neurological make-up of the brain. For example, imaginative and creative play is known to lower levels of stress chemicals, enabling children to deal more successfully with stressful situations. Gentle rough and tumble play and laughter are also known to have anti-stress effects, activating the brain's emotion-regulating centres and causing the release of opioids, the natural brain chemicals that induce feelings of pleasure and well-being (Sunderland 2006).

Play during childhood can stimulate a 'playful' approach to life at a later age, including the ability to bring humour and fun to relationships and to see life's difficulties as challenges rather than insurmountable obstacles. It helps children to develop social awareness and conscience and creates opportunities to explore concepts of fairness and equality.

I like David Cohen's exclamation: 'Ponder the irony! Children are the experts at play, play is their work and yet we, long-out-of-practice oldies, think we can teach them how to play!' (Cohen 1993, p.13) and Vivian Paley's expansion on this: 'We were taught to say that play is the work of children. But watching and listening to them, I saw that play was nothing less than Truth and Life.' (Paley 1991, p.17)

Games provide structure and predictability

How do games fit into this magical world of play? Garvey defines games as play activities that are structured with 'explicit rules that can be precisely communicated' (1977, p.101).

The ability to play games with rules usually emerges at around five or six years of age although, as outlined above, the early signs of this can be seen with very young infants (a game of peek-a-boo for example involves structured turn-taking to some extent and children of three often understand the 'unspoken' rules of familiar games). By around five years of age children are more able to tolerate waiting and a degree of inevitable frustration at being 'out' in a competitive game. They are beginning to exercise self-control and the ability to follow rules and conventions. They are also more able to sustain interactions with others for longer periods.

Games generally have clear start and finishing points and follow sequences which are accepted by the players and which can therefore be replicated at other times and in different situations. These 'process' rules provide a sense of predictability and security even when the game itself might be a bit scary, and in this way various events and situations which might be too difficult or painful to confront head on can be played out in safety. Such games engender laughter and enjoyment whilst dealing with important life issues.

Opie and Opie conducted extensive research into children's street games in the 1960s. They observed that:

> Children like games in which there is a sizeable element of luck, so that individual abilities cannot be directly compared. They like games which restart almost automatically, so that everybody is given a new chance. They like games

which move in stages, in which each stage, the choosing of leaders, the picking-up of sides, the determining of which child shall start, is almost a game in itself…many of the games, particularly those of young children, are more akin to ceremonies than competitions. In these games children gain the reassurance that comes with repetition, and the feeling of fellowship that comes from doing the same as everyone else. (Opie and Opie in Bruner *et al.* 1976, pp.394–5)

Interestingly, a study carried out by Roberts and Sutton-Smith in 1962 found evidence of an association between the type of games played (whether they were predominantly based on strategy, skill or luck) and the type of upbringing of different groups of children (where the emphasis was placed on responsibility, achievement or obedience). Whatever the main orientation of games might be, however, they all provide children with the opportunity to explore the function of rules and conventions and to safely test the boundaries of what is acceptable to others within a fun and rewarding but nevertheless rule-governed activity.

In their daily lives children have to negotiate their way through a welter of adult-imposed rules, structures and boundaries. Sometimes these are explicit but often they are unclear or unspoken, taken for granted by the adults but a potential minefield for children who forget, don't know or don't understand them. Constant insistence on adherence to adult imposed rules in games may similarly have a negative effect on the process, resulting in children disengaging with the games, rebelling or becoming passive. Rules should therefore be flexible enough to accommodate different types or levels of response.

A major way in which children will learn to understand and respect rules is by having experience of devising them for themselves, preferably by negotiating with others, and then trying them out. In this way they learn that games are usually only successful when everyone adheres to the rules but that there can also be differing versions and perspectives. They learn that they have choices and that others will listen to their ideas.

Games reflect aspects of real life. The ways in which children engage in them often reflects their approach to life in general

As mindful facilitators of the game process, we can make certain hypotheses about the ways in which children participate in structured games. First, the way a child acts and reacts in a game situation is likely to reflect her life experiences in some way and therefore also reflect how she behaves in other situations. So, without being overly analytical or too literal in our interpretations of children's behaviour during play it is nevertheless important for us to be aware of general patterns. Are there children who take a long time to warm up to each game? Are there some who are 'taking over'?

What happens when children become frustrated or cannot tolerate waiting their turn? Are they able to recognize personal achievements and those of others? Do they behave independently or always look to others to take the lead? Are they able to take on different roles at different times or for different types of game?

A second hypothesis that we might make centres on children's capacity for change. Working within a humanistic framework, we can approach the playing of games with the assumption that all children, whatever their current abilities, have within them the resources, and therefore the potential, for change and growth. However small or large the changes might be, the ability to respond with a degree of flexibility in different situations and the ability to learn from active participation is part of what it is to be human.

Finally, we should also remember that each child's attitude to different games, his degree of participation and his enjoyment of the game will change over time as he matures and learns.

Games provide valuable learning opportunities in many different areas of social and personal development

Games not only provide a means to address issues that have already been identified as causing some difficulties but can also be played in a proactive way to prevent future problems from occurring. In the context of this book, they can be viewed as providing steps towards building and maintaining successful social skills; steps that need to be continually repeated and reinforced in order to have maximum effect.

Figure 3.1 gives an indication of just some of the many specific and more general learning opportunities available to children through structured games sessions.

Undoubtedly, there are many more aspects that could be added according to the orientation of the group (family group, class, occupational therapy group, speech and language therapy group, after school group etc.). The following chapter explores issues specifically related to working with groups and in particular to the responsibility of adults in regard to structuring the emotional environment.

Specific learning/consolidation of skills

Developing spoken language skills

Developing listening skills

Developing observation skills

Ability to follow complex instructions

Ability to be reflective

Developing memory skills

Ability to give instructions

Creating new rules and conventions

Ability to take turns and tolerate waiting

Developing problem-solving skills

Developing skills of cooperation

Developing self-responsibility and leadership skills

Building the ability to persist with an activity

Making mistakes in a safe environment

Developing ability to acknowledge others' actions and give feedback

Development of body image and body awareness

Understanding the different functions of games

Understanding and exploring different types of games

Using communication skills appropriately for context

Developing ability to select and modify games and rules appropriately

Learning through 'doing' not 'producing'

Exploring social and cultural aspects of games

Learning how games can reinforce previous learning

Recognizing that learning can span several subjects at once

Promoting the idea that learning is fun

Understanding rules that are made by someone else

Understanding how rules are made

Personal/social learning ———————— ———————— Process learning

Building self-respect and respect of others

Understanding concepts of tolerance, fairness and empathy

Understanding concept of responsibility for own actions and how behaviour affects others

Recognizing and understanding emotions

Tolerating frustration and building emotional resilience

Reducing impulsivity and building persistence

Exploring links between thoughts, actions and feelings

Developing sensitivity to other people's strengths and difficulties

Building confidence

Building self-efficacy

Extending conscious awareness

Exploring self-concept

Building trust

Learning about the social value of individual achievements

Learning to be flexible in thought and action

Thinking independently and imaginatively

Transferable skills

Changes in attitudes or beliefs as result of learning from the social context of games

Reaching an understanding of complex experiences through a non-threatening medium

Devising own games as a result of understanding the general rules about the structure and content of games

Non-specific learning/consolidation of skills

Figure 3.1 Learning opportunities available to children through structured games

Structuring the emotional environment

Key concepts

- The core conditions of empathy, unconditional positive regard and congruence proposed by Carl Rogers offer an important framework for supporting the development of social skills.

- Roles, rules and boundaries need to be clearly defined so that children feel safe.

- A nurturing environment is one in which all emotions are acknowledged and valued.

- It is important to value each child for simply being who they are and to ensure that he or she actually experiences this positive regard.

- Praise is most effective when it is specific and realistic.

- A solution-focused approach helps children to recognize their skills, strengths and resources.

The core conditions of empathy, unconditional positive regard and congruence proposed by Carl Rogers offer an important framework for supporting the development of social skills

Carl Rogers, the originator of 'person-centred' therapy, believed that each individual will naturally strive to achieve his or her full potential in life and proposed that there are certain conditions which will promote this tendency. These became known as the 'core conditions' for a successful therapeutic alliance but Rogers also made it clear that he believed such conditions were valid for all human relationships. He hypothesized that if he maintained a relationship characterized on his part by congruence ('a genuineness and transparency, in which I am my real feelings'), unconditional positive regard ('warm acceptance of and prizing of the other person as a separate individual') and empathy ('a sensitive ability to see his world and himself as he sees them') then the other person in the relationship:

will experience and understand aspects of himself which previously he has repressed;

will find himself becoming better integrated, more able to function effectively;

will become more similar to the person he would like to be;

will be more self-directing and self-confident;

will become more of a person, more unique and more self-expressive;

will be more understanding, more acceptant of others;

will be able to cope with the problems of life more adequately and more comfortably. (Rogers 1961, pp.37–8)

In practical terms facilitators can demonstrate these core conditions in a number of ways. The following areas should all be given careful consideration:

- roles, rules and boundaries
- understanding and valuing emotions
- praising
- self-reflection.

Self-reflection is covered in Chapter 6. The next section looks at each of the other three elements in turn and explores them in relation to playing games in groups. However, although the focus is on group interactions, the principles apply just as much to playing games with individual children or within families.

Roles, rules and boundaries need to be clearly defined so that children feel safe

For some children, new games can be scary and we need to spend time building trust amongst group members and between ourselves and the children we are supporting. Trust is most easily established if roles, rules and boundaries are clearly outlined at the start of a group. This can help children to feel 'contained' and safe. An example of a clear time boundary might be:

'Today the games session will be 10 minutes long and when we have finished the game we will do X'

Or:

'Every morning we will play one game during circle time and then we will…'

Further guidelines on setting the focus for games can be found in Chapter 1, particularly the section headed *Integrating games into different settings* (p.18).

It is also the facilitator's task to demonstrate a firm but fair approach in order to prevent difficulties arising for example from children being consistently very dominant or ridiculed by others because they do not understand the game rules. It is crucial that all group members (including family groups) understand the importance of supporting each other's participation – even games that purport to be non-competitive can sometimes be played in a competitive, even aggressive way unless there are clear guidelines. Again, this will enable the children to feel safe within the structure of the games and allow them the opportunity to experiment and explore; to expand their self-concept and to self-evaluate without fear of being judged harshly.

Because of the multi-faceted nature of games there will be multiple roles for those who choose to coordinate games sessions with young children. It is important to decide which roles you are taking on. Although these may change and evolve over time, deciding on your role and the purpose of the games you choose will help you to structure and reflect on the sessions more effectively. Possible roles might include several of the following at any one time:

- role model
- teacher/provider of challenges
- facilitator/encourager/enabler
- supporter/helper
- mediator/arbitrator
- observer
- participant
- researcher/information gatherer/assessor
- supervisor
- provider of fun
- ideas person
- time keeper.

Consider whether or not the roles you are taking on conflict in any way and if so, which one you need to concentrate on. Perhaps a second person is needed to take a different perspective or role? For example, can you be facilitator/encourager and also record information about how individuals are coping with different aspects of a particular game?

In which role are you happiest? Do you feel most comfortable as 'provider of fun' or most comfortable in the 'teaching' role?

What about the roles of the children? These too may change and evolve over time so that group members each have the opportunity to be the game coordinator or the 'ideas' person or 'teacher'. Those who feel unable to join in with a particular game may enjoy being timekeeper or observer. Children who understand the rules of games and can explain these to others may naturally take on the role of arbitrator or game coordinator, leading others in making choices and in ensuring that the rules are understood and followed by all participants. This is a valuable skill which can be facilitated during many of the games suggested in this book.

Monitoring of games by the participants themselves is an important aspect of play. Children who would normally find this role difficult can be gradually encouraged and supported in leading and monitoring fairly. Those children who have plenty of experience in arbitrating and leading games can also be encouraged to support this process by stepping back to allow others to have a go.

Games sessions also need 'rules' or guidelines to help foster the feeling of trust and safety amongst those taking part. Formulating ground rules for groups who are specifically working on social skills helps to ensure that the group is a safe place to be. Two of the most important rules for facilitators to make clear are:

1.   *Children will always be given the choice of staying in or out of the game.*
      For children who opt out frequently you may want to suggest an
      alternative role such as timekeeper to encourage some initial involvement.
      For some anxious children, observing others engaging in a game without
      feeling in any way included could allow the build-up of negative
      emotions, whereas for others it gives them the opportunity to prepare
      themselves to join in by watching what happens and familiarizing
      themselves with the rules.

2.   *Children who are reluctant to take part straight away may choose to join in at any
      time by giving a signal.*

Note: If the group appears generally restless do not insist on continuing for a certain number of set rounds of a game, take it as an indication that it is not the right time to play this game or that it is not the right game for this group.

Further rules should be established for the reflection/discussion time. In order for children to feel comfortable in contributing to these sessions they need to know that their ideas and opinions are valued and that they will be listened to without judgement from others and without being interrupted. Older children should also be encouraged to explore differing opinions where appropriate, thus giving them the opportunity to debate a point constructively.

A nurturing environment is one in which all emotions are acknowledged and valued

In games, children who have difficulty in understanding and expressing their feelings verbally, can begin to explore difficult emotions in safety and with the spirit of 'play'. In this way, games help children to recognize that others often have similar experiences and emotions. However, we should also be aware that when children are in groups together, they will all have feelings about the feelings of the other children! Displays of anxiety, anger or upset by one child may trigger feelings of anxiety, anger or distress in another. It will be the facilitator's task to help children to regulate their emotions within the group and demonstrate a calm way of reacting to any displays of strong emotion.

How do we help children to be constructively aware of their emotions? The key is to acknowledge and validate feelings. For example, if a child with a hearing difficulty says 'I hate this game, it's stupid,' think about the feeling behind the comment. Avoid interpretations but comment on what you see, hear and feel. Aim to support rather than rescue. Responses such as, 'But everyone else is enjoying it, I'm sure you will too,' 'You haven't tried it yet, let's have a go together,' or 'That's OK, you can sit this one out if you like' would probably all get a negative reaction. Such comments, whilst well-meaning, do not help the child to understand his own feelings more fully or to discover his own solutions in situations that he finds difficult (see p.41 for further exploration of solution-focused talk).

Making a hypothesis about the feeling behind the words and offering an appropriate comment ('It's a very noisy game and I noticed that it's hard to hear the instructions sometimes. I wonder if it would be more fun for you to stand nearer the teacher') can help the child to feel understood and is more likely to lead to him making adjustments in his self-evaluation.

It is important to value each child for simply being who they are and to ensure that he or she actually experiences this positive regard

A clear demonstration that we value each child as a unique individual can have far-reaching effects and yet can be conveyed to children in the simplest of ways, for example by making sure that each child in the group has been acknowledged by name as they arrive, and by giving some indication of pleasure that they are there (a smile, a 'thumbs up' gesture). Telling a child that we enjoy her company, or love talking with her emphasizes the fact that she has a positive 'effect' on us simply by being who she is and not because of what she does or doesn't say or do.

Individual differences in social customs, beliefs and behaviours should also be acknowledged and an atmosphere of open discussion should be encouraged. Children need to feel safe enough to be able to say what is the 'norm' for their family or culture when this differs from the general consensus of the group.

Praise is most effective when it is specific and realistic

Praise and demonstration of pleasure in a child's abilities, perseverance, sense of fun etc. can be an excellent motivator for continued change and development, but it will be of little value if it is not genuine or has no personal meaning for the child. If praise does not resonate with his self-concept and self-evaluations he is very likely to reject it. Also, unrealistic or unjustified praise could set him up for experiencing low self-esteem if he tries to do things before he is ready or if it leads to him developing unrealistically high expectations of what he can achieve. Unfortunately, even when adults do offer genuine praise this can so frequently be followed by a qualification of some sort, negating the praise completely. Such qualified praise might go something like:

> 'What a great way to share – if only you'd done that this morning you wouldn't have got into a fight!'

> 'Well done for sticking to the rules – why can't you always do that without getting grumpy?'

> 'I noticed that you were being really helpful when Sam was upset – you'd usually get cross with him wouldn't you?'

Similarly, it can be all too easy to offer praise that indicates the lesser achievements of others. An award for the fastest worker or best listener for example, suggests that there are others in the group who are not so good at this and also gives little scope for further development (If I am already the best, I don't need to think about that any more!).

The most effective approach is to use genuine specific, descriptive praise whenever possible: 'I liked the way you really listened to what Josh had to say about following the rules of the game,' 'I noticed you were being very helpful when Sam got upset and that really worked because he calmed down straight away!'

Sometimes it is also helpful to acknowledge difficulties and empathize with the feelings: 'It looked like it was hard for you to wait your turn. You had lots of great ideas to share! That must have been really frustrating for you!'

Model and encourage realistic, positive praise: 'What did you like about the way that Josh handled that?' Encourage older children to reflect on what happens within games, picking up on the encounters and strategies that are working well and in particular, any moments of difficulty which have been successfully negotiated. Use memory aids if necessary to remember what children have done in previous games sessions. Non-judgemental comments on past experiences and actions can be extremely motivating and self-affirming for children.

Non-verbal signals of approval and encouragement can also be very effective. A 'thumbs up', a wink or a smile across a room can all indicate to a child that you have noticed them without drawing the attention of other children in the group – this sort of 'private' praise is particularly helpful for children who are anxious and may be enough to break the train of thought that could lead to withdrawal or displays of frustration.

Christine Durham, in her book *Chasing Ideas* (Durham 2006) describes a wonderful way to make praise a fun interaction. She suggests the use of acronyms and abbreviations such as VIP (very important proposition) or IT (insightful thinking). For older children, this could start as a game in itself – perhaps taking familiar acronyms and familiar sayings and encouraging group members to make up 'secret' messages about behaviour and thoughts that are specific to social skills. For example VIP could be 'Very Imaginative Problem-Solver' or ACE could be 'A Cool Example'. Giving a child a 'thumbs up' sign and saying 'ACE' then becomes even more meaningful and fun!

A solution-focused approach helps children to recognize their skills, strengths and resources

When children are having difficulty in changing behaviour and thought patterns, engaging them in solution-focused strategies can be extremely useful. Solution-focused brief therapy (SFBT) is a recognized therapeutic and teaching approach. As its name suggests, this approach encourages solution-based, rather than problem-based dialogue. Some of the basic assumptions and styles of interaction inherent in SFBT are easily incorporated into daily contacts with children and can make a big difference to how a child begins to see herself and the possibility of change.

In essence, solution-focused communication arises quite naturally from a philosophy that emphasizes the skills, strengths and resources of individuals. If we believe that a child is capable of change, that he has the resources for change and he doesn't always need to be told what to do, then our communications will reflect this.

Solution-focused language also reflects the assumption that the child will already be doing something that will help him towards his goal, however small that step might be. Let's take the example used earlier of a child with a hearing impairment not wanting to join in with games. If this child is evidently frustrated and angry, an individual discussion after the games session might go something like this:

Child: I hate these games.

Adult: Sometimes you really hate the games we're playing.

Child: Yeah. No one ever listens to me (kicks the table leg forcefully).

(*The use of words like 'never', 'always' and 'no one' adds justification to the anger: if no one ever takes any notice of me then I am justified in feeling angry.*)

Adult: Some people don't listen to you and then you get angry.

(*Anger is acknowledged and deliberately linked with a particular trigger in order to suggest an alternative to the sense of constant anger.*)

Child: Yeah!

Adult: So when we're playing these games and you're *not* angry, how does that feel?

(*This introduces the idea of the exception to the rule.*)

Child: Dunno. OK I guess.

Adult: You feel OK sometimes. I wonder what will be different when you are feeling OK in the games more often?

(*This assumes that the change will happen and helps the child to begin to 'flesh out' the details of what that will be like and what they will do in order to make it happen. The more details 'the preferred future' can be given, the more likely it is to happen.*)

In this shortened version of a possible interaction the adult has acknowledged the problem but has introduced the possibility for change by using words like 'sometimes' and by looking for the exception to the feeling of constant anger. It is important for the child to focus on what they *will* be feeling, doing and thinking not on what they *don't* want. Other questions might therefore include:

What else will you notice?

How will your teacher / classmates know that you are feeling OK?

What will happen then?

In summary, there are several key points to consider when we are helping children to develop social skills. We need to:

- be curious about how he views himself (his theory about who he is)
- be fully aware of how our actions and words affect his self-concept and therefore his feelings of self-worth and competency
- show genuine warmth and respect for him as a unique individual
- show him that he can make mistakes in social situations and still be loved and valued
- help him to develop self-awareness and realization of how his behaviour affects other people
- help him to understand that emotions can change in form and intensity according to many different factors and that this is normal but that it need not be an overwhelming or scary experience.

Significantly, these are very similar to the key issues that are involved in supporting the development and maintenance of healthy self-esteem (Plummer 2007a, 2007b).

5

Transfer and maintenance of skills

In Chapter 4 we explored how games can provide a powerful learning experience for children at various stages of their development. For older children, discussions about what happened during a game can greatly enhance the learning process but in some instances, further support may still be needed. The following suggestions draw on a range of cognitive and behavioural strategies to reinforce the appropriate use of skills in new or challenging situations and will be particularly useful for children who may already be feeling isolated because of difficulties with social interactions. Above all else, the building and  maintenance of social skills will be most effective when a partnership approach to learning is established. When children, carers, professionals and support staff work together to identify areas of need and existing strengths then the carry-over from structured activities to more general behaviour is much more likely.

Modelling, shaping and reinforcement

The shaping of desired behaviours occurs quite naturally even when we are not specifically targeting these. Children learn acceptable behaviour from the models around them and will be rewarded in some form (perhaps by increased attention or direct verbal feedback) for positive social behaviour. *Specific* shaping however, involves identifying the basic features of a skill and rewarding successive steps towards building that skill. This means that we have to be on the alert to spot actual moments of appropriate behaviour or indications of appropriate thinking in order to give realistic and specific feedback (see notes on praise in Chapter 4: Structuring the emotional environment, p.40). Such praise and feedback can do much to motivate a child to persevere with their learning but we should be aware that it can also be 'over-done' and loose its potency. Realistic self-evaluation and self-reward should therefore also be encouraged so that there is a healthy balance between these two processes.

In order for both the intrinsic and extrinsic reinforcement of skills to have maximum effect we also need to think about the relevance of particular skills for individual children. A child is much more likely to be motivated to learn and use social skills if they can see the personal benefits of doing so.

Setting realistic and relevant targets

Children need plenty of opportunities to practise the skills that they are developing but such opportunities need to be carefully structured in order to avoid the risk of repeated failure because the target was perhaps too high or too vague. For instance, a child who has problems with attention control may need help in focusing on language with minimal distractions or conversely, may need visual prompts such as picture cards to help him to stay focused. A child who has difficulty in imagining another person's point of view may need to start with tasks such as imagining what her bedroom would like if it were painted a different colour, or what her day would be like if she were a giant or an animal, before she can imagine what it might be like for her classmate to be upset.

Setting realistic targets also means that we need to provide children with the opportunity to explore a range of skills and responses so that they have choices about which skills are most relevant for them to use for different situations.

Stories

Stories that explore different social situations can be an invaluable tool for promoting awareness of social competence. These could be commercially produced stories or stories that the children have invented individually or that have been produced jointly with an adult or in a peer group. There are many books for children of all ages which explore emotions and different social encounters such as being bullied, meeting new people and 'performing' in front of peers. A brief description of some of those that I have found most useful can be found in the Appendix.

Drama techniques

Drama techniques are widely used in schools and are similar to some strategies used in *drama therapy*. Although the following outlines are not descriptions of therapy strategies, even at this level of use it is important to make sure that the children have stepped out of role after completion of the activity. The release of role can be done by simple means such as asking the children to name and put away any props they have used and by getting them to shake their arms and hands and call out their own name, or count to three and turn round.

Role play

Carefully structured role play provides opportunities for practice which can be particularly useful for a child who would otherwise have limited chances to try out new skills. Role play involves setting up imaginary situations where children can be given instant feedback on their successes and offered ideas on how to expand on their current skills. Because these situations are staged, the role play can be stopped at any point in order to bring in new elements, swap roles or draw attention to specific aspects of the interaction.

Hot seating

This encourages children to explore aspects of empathizing with another person's point of view or feelings. The group listens to a short story or a description of an event. One child sits in the 'hot-seat' in role as one of the characters from the story. The rest of the group are invited to ask this person questions in order to explore perceived feelings and situations from the character's perspective. Questions can be spontaneous or briefly planned beforehand.

Tunnel of thoughts

(Also known as conscience alley or decision alley.)

The group form two lines facing each other. One person takes on the role of a character in a story that is faced with a decision or dilemma. This character walks down the centre of the tunnel as the rest of the group speak out thoughts in support of both sides of the decision (e.g. I should listen to this person because___, I should walk away from this person because ___). The character, having consulted his 'conscience' in this way, has choice about what thoughts to take on board and what to discard. He then makes his decision on reaching the end of the tunnel.

Thought bubbling

(Also known as thought tracking.)

This is another way of encouraging empathic responses by exploring the 'private' thoughts of a character, usually at a point of crisis or dilemma in a story. One person takes on the role of the character and the rest of the group stand in a circle around her and take turns to 'speak the thought' that the character might be having at that particular point in the story. These thoughts might be different to or the same as the thoughts that the character is actually speaking.

This can also be done in pairs, where two people take on the same character role and speak two different perspectives while the rest of the group ask questions about their actions and choices.

Paired improvisation

Two people take on the roles of two different characters in a story and have a conversation for a pre-set period of time and with no prior planning.

Turn around theatre

(Suitable for 9–12 players per scenario.)

The success of this activity rests on the ability of group members to 'tune in' to each other and to work spontaneously as a team. The group is divided into three smaller subgroups who will act out the beginning, middle and end of a given scenario e.g. 'You are with a group of friends walking home from school and you see a new member of your class being bullied by some older children.' The first subgroup is given a few minutes to sort out roles. They then perform the first part of the play while the other groups watch. At an appropriate point the second group take over and elaborate on the story. It is up to the third group to act out a suitable resolution to the situation.

Recognizing and changing self-talk

Self-talk is the 'story' that we tell ourselves about who we are, how we feel and what we are able or not able to do. This story will affect how we behave, how we learn and how we relate to other people. If a child is shunned by classmates because of her social ineptness then her internal monologue might be something like 'I can't make friends. Nobody likes me. Everyone thinks I'm stupid…' The 'all or nothing' nature of this self-talk – can't, nobody, everyone – and the fact that it is in the present tense give an all-pervading sense of hopelessness, as if these perceptions and feelings are unalterable facts. The story that she is telling herself may well become a self-fulfilling prophecy as she continues to build images of herself as a 'useless person that nobody likes'. These images in turn will inform the way that she relates to others in the future.

This interaction of images, thoughts and behaviour can be altered however. So, for example, if a child changes the story that she tells herself, she will gradually change the subconscious images that inform her behaviour and begin to act in ways that are congruent with her new thoughts and beliefs. A solution-focused dialogue is one way of encouraging changes in self-talk (see pp.41–2). Solution-focused brief therapy (SFBT) also fits very comfortably with the use of imagery for helping children to talk about things in a way that is one step removed from the painful experiences or difficulties they are facing.

Imagework

There are many approaches to helping children to work with their images in a constructive way, for example, in the form of guided journeys or stories where children are encouraged to interact with the characters and objects that they meet and to create their own images to represent problems, dilemmas and questions (Plummer 1999).

Adults can also offer images if it seems appropriate – 'When you were really angry with Sam just now, I got this image of a tiger that had been hurt. Is that how you felt?' or 'This problem seems like a huge lump of rock to me – we just can't seem to shift it. What could we do about this rock?' Children are often more than willing to put you right and to suggest their own images if they think you haven't quite grasped the essence of what they are feeling: 'No, its more like a big swampy puddle...!' Simply talking about images in this way can often enable a child to see solutions or can precipitate a shift in perception where none seemed possible before (Plummer 2007a).

By providing children with the means to foster creative use of their imagination we can help them to build a unified sense of their inner and outer worlds; help them to see events, problems and challenges from a different viewpoint; and enable them to find the way forward that is most appropriate for their individual needs.

Problem-solving activities

As with all areas of learning, children will tend to generalize social skills more readily if they have had plenty of opportunities to engage in problem-solving activities. It is important to remember that some children learn best with visual or auditory prompts, others need to physically engage in an activity. For example, you could set the task of mastering a trick such as how to tie a knot in a piece of string without letting go of either end of the string (you have to start with your arms folded!). The children then have to explain to another group how to do it (without actually showing them) so that this second group can demonstrate it successfully. The whole group then work out what skills were needed in order both to solve the problem and to teach the trick to someone else.

In relation to problem-solving real-life interactions, the most common format is:

1. Identify the problem clearly and concisely.

2. Brainstorm as many solutions as possible, including any that might seem untenable.

3. Look at the consequences of each of the possibilities.

4. Choose the most useful strategies.

5. Try out one of the strategies.

6. Evaluate the outcome.

7. Keep, discard or alter the strategy in light of the evaluation.

Mentors

Group members can be allocated a 'mentee' for a specific period of time (a games session, a day, a week). During this time they keep an eye out for their protégé and offer praise and encouragement, or support in other pre-defined ways. All group members should have the chance to be both mentor and mentee. This works well in families where a younger child can feel that they have something positive to contribute to another family member's learning. Because there is a time limit on this there is also less chance of an individual stepping in too much and deskilling a child rather than supporting them.

Diaries, wikis and blogs

Older children who are learning IT skills may like to engage in setting up a blog (internet diary) where they can report on their own successes, or better still, a group wiki which other members of the group can contribute to. A wiki (collaborative website) allows children to make collaborative contributions and to ask each other questions, share experiences etc. The children should know that this will be monitored by the group facilitator. It is a particularly helpful tool for the transfer and maintenance of skills where group members are unable to meet up between sessions.

6

Self-reflection and self-care

Key concepts

- The reflective process helps us
  ensure that the support we
  offer to children is timely and
  effective.

- Games are fun!

The reflective process helps us ensure that
the support we offer to children is timely
and effective

The importance of being reflective lies
in the way that we use this skill to
develop the most effective way of facilitating change in ourselves and in others.
In the context of social skills we obviously need to be aware of our own feelings and
needs and the way in which what we do and say has a direct effect on the children in
our care.

One aspect to be particularly aware of is how we cope with groups and monitor
group processes. Larger groups will undoubtedly benefit from having at least two
facilitators. It is very difficult to 'hold' a group and to be aware of everything that is
going on within and between all the group members if you are working on your own.
Having two facilitators gives you the chance to share ideas, keep better track of what
is happening and obviously share the responsibility for planning, carrying out and
evaluating the sessions.

It is also important for each facilitator to be able to reflect on his or her skills as a
group leader and to be able to debrief at the end of each session. This is much harder
if you are only able to do this infrequently with a peer or at a scheduled supervision
session.

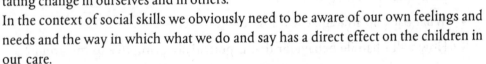

Taking time to reflect on the group process and on the session can enable facilitators to deal with the challenges and joys of a group more effectively and to monitor facilitation skills in ways that are most likely to support the children. An added bonus of course is that constructive discussions with a co-facilitator help to strengthen personal feelings of competency and self-worth.

With regard to the process of games sessions there are also a few areas to think about. The following questions are some that I have found helpful when planning and reviewing sessions:

- What is my role as the game coordinator?
- How will I set the tone of the session/introduce the games in a fun way?
- Why are we playing these particular games? What are my aims/intended outcomes?
- How will I know if I've achieved my aims/outcomes?
- What are my personal feelings about these games?
- Are the games appropriate for the age/cultural background of the children in the group?
- Do I know the 'rules' of the games?
- Who (if anyone) in the group will find the games difficult/challenging/easy?
- Do I need to adapt the games in any way to allow/encourage full participation of all group members?
- What back up strategies will I need?
- How will I handle behaviour that is potentially disruptive to the group?
- Am I aware of why this behaviour might occur?
- If the group is large or diverse in needs do I have a 'support' person available?
- What will I do if a child knows a different version of a game and wants to play that? (For example, you might suggest that you play their version next time or it might be appropriate to share different versions at the time and abandon one of the other games you had planned.)
- Is this the right time for the game(s)?
- Is the room the right temperature?
- Am I feeling up to it?

Games are fun!

After completion of a games session it is useful to take a few moments as soon as you can to reflect on the game(s) you chose to play. What went well? Was there anything that was difficult to monitor? What skills did you use? What did you enjoy about the games? What did the children most enjoy? Remember, reflective practice is not about being judgemental about our own abilities. It is about reflecting on our skills and on our learning and on our ways of navigating any difficulties.

So, the theory finished with, let's get going and *play some games!*

Bibliography

Antidote (2003) *The Emotional Literacy Handbook: Promoting Whole-School Strategies.* London: David Fulton Publishers.

Arnold, A. (1976) *The World Book of Children's Games.* London: Pan Books Ltd.

Beswick, C. (2003) *The Little Book of Parachute Play.* Husbands Bosworth: Featherstone Education Ltd.

Brandes, D. and Phillips, H. (1979) *Gamesters' Handbook. 140 Games for Teachers and Group Leaders.* London: Hutchinson.

Bruner, J.S., Jolly, A. and Sylva, K. (eds) (1976) *Play: Its Role in Development and Evolution.* Harmondsworth: Penguin.

DfES (2005) Social and emotional aspects of learning. Primary National Strategy.

Eliot, L. (1999) *What's Going on in There? How the Brain and Mind Develop in the First Five Years of Life.* New York: Bantam.

Ellis, M.J. (1973) *Why People Play.* Englewood Cliffs, NJ: Prentice Hall, Inc.

Liebmann, M. (2004) *Art Therapy for Groups. A Handbook of Themes and Exercises* (2nd edition). London and New York: Routledge.

Masheder, M. (1989) *Let's Play Together.* London: Green Print.

Neelands, J. (1990) *Structuring Drama Work. A Handbook of Available Forms in Theatre and Drama.* Cambridge: Cambridge University Press.

References

Bandura, A. (1977) 'Self-efficacy: Towards a unifying theory of behavioural change.' *Psychological Review 84,* 191–215.

Carpendale, J. and Lewis, C. (2006) *How Children Develop Social Understanding.* Oxford: Blackwell Publishing.

Cohen, D. (1993) *The Development of Play* (2nd edition). London: Routledge.

DCSF (2007) *The Children's Plan: Building brighter futures – Summary.* Norwich: TSO (The Stationery Office). Available at www.dcsf.gov.uk/publications/childrensplan, accessed 12 June 2008.

Durham, C. (2006) *Chasing Ideas.* London and Philadelphia: Jessica Kingsley Publishers.

Garvey, C. (1977) *Play.* London: Fontana/Open Books.

Gerhardt, S. (2004) *Why Love Matters. How Affection Shapes a Baby's Brain.* London and New York: Routledge.

Goleman, D. (1996) *Emotional Intelligence. Why It Can Matter More than IQ.* London: Bloomsbury.

Harter, S. (1999) *The Construction of the Self.* New York: Guilford Press.

Lalonde, C.E. and Chandler, M.J. (1995) 'False belief understanding goes to school: On the social-emotional consequences of coming early or late to a first theory of mind.' *Cognition and Emotion 9,* 167–185.

Nowicki, S. and Duke, M. (1992) *Helping the Child Who Doesn't Fit In.* Atlanta: Peachtree Publishers Ltd.

Opie, I. and Opie, P. (1976) Street Games: 'Counting-out and Chasing.' In J.S. Bruner, A. Jolly and K. Sylva (eds) *Play – Its Role in Development and Evolution.* Harmondsworth: Penguin.

Paley, V.G. (1991) *The Boy Who Would be a Helicopter.* London: Harvard University Press.

Plummer, D. (1999) *Using Interactive Imagework with Children: Walking on the Magic Mountain.* London and Philadelphia: Jessica Kingsley Publishers.

Plummer, D. (2007a) *Helping Children to Build Self-Esteem.* (2nd edition). London and Philadelphia: Jessica Kingsley Publishers.

Plummer, D. (2007b) *Self-Esteem Games for Children.* London and Philadelphia: Jessica Kingsley Publishers.

Plummer, D. (2008) *Anger Management Games for Children.* London and Philadelphia: Jessica Kingsley Publishers.

Roberts, J.M. and Sutton-Smith, B. (1962) 'Child training and game involvement.' *Ethnology* *1*, 166–85.

Rogers, C.R. (1961) *On Becoming a Person: A Therapist's View of Psychotherapy.* London: Constable.

Rogers, C.R. (1980) *A Way of Being.* Boston: Houghton Mifflin.

Sunderland, M. (2006) *The Science of Parenting.* London: Dorling Kindersley.

Part Two

Games for social skills

As with any games involving the use of equipment, the parachute games outlined in this book should be supervised by an adult at all times. Small children can easily get themselves tangled up in a large parachute – at the very least this can be a very scary experience for them.

Explanatory notes for the adaptation and reflection sections of games are provided on pages 17–18. The symbols used for each game are also repeated here for ease of reference:

⑤	This gives an indication of the suggested *youngest* age for playing the game. There is no upper age limit.
⏰ 10 mins	An approximate time is suggested for the length of the game (excluding the discussion time). This will obviously vary according to the size of the group and the ability of the players.
♦ ♦ ♦	Indicates that the game is suitable for larger groups (eight or more).
♦ ♦	The game is suitable for small groups.
ᗑᗑᗑ	The game involves a lot of speaking unless it is adapted.
ᗑᗑ	A moderate amount of speaking is required by players.
ᗑ	The game is primarily a non-verbal game or one requiring minimal speech.
☑ empathy	This gives an indication of a foundation ability or skill used or developed by playing this game.

7

Non-competitive ways
to choose groups and group leaders

It is worth having several different methods of dividing players into groups or pairs or choosing someone to lead a game. For the purpose of these games we want to avoid placing children in a position where they are anxiously waiting to be 'picked' or where the same groups or pairs consistently choose to work together. The following methods are just some of the many ways in which to encourage random selections.

To choose a leader

- Have names in a hat or in separate balloons. Players pick a name or pop a balloon to see who is the leader for that session. This ensures that everyone gets a turn eventually.

- Take turns according to dates of birth (e.g. using just the date in the month).

To choose pairs

- Count round half the circle then start again. The 'one's work together, 'two's work together, etc.

- Put two sets of matching objects in a 'lucky dip' box. Players draw out an object and find their partner who has a matching object.

- Players stand in a circle with eyes closed and arms outstretched. They walk across the circle until they meet someone else.

To choose groups

- Sit in a large circle. Count round in sets of two or four or however many small groups are needed. '*One*'s then work together, '*two*'s work together, etc.

- Count round the circle using colour names, with as many different colours as are needed for the number of groups.

- Deal out playing cards e.g. all the clubs in one group and diamonds in the other.

8

Getting to know each other: warm-ups and ice-breakers

A reminder:

Before you begin to play games with a new group, don't forget to establish the basic ground rules. *The rule of the realm* (p. 147) is a useful game to play in order to introduce a discussion about these.

Parachute name game

⑤
🕐 10 mins
♁ ♁
💬

☑ listening
☑ memory
☑ taking turns
☑ concentration

☑ observation

With a little imagination, many games can be adapted to include the use of a parachute. Parachute games are fun for children of all ages and provide an excellent focus for outdoor play.

How to play　Players hold the parachute at waist level. A large soft ball is placed in the middle of the parachute. The game coordinator says the name of each player in turn and everyone tries to send the ball across the circle to that person.

Adaptation　Players crouch down around the outside of the parachute, holding tightly to the edge. The game coordinator says, 'one two three up parachute' and everyone jumps up, making the parachute mushroom into the air. The coordinator quickly calls the names of two players who must swap places by running underneath the parachute before it floats back down.

Reflection　Our names are a very important part of who we are. How do we hear our names used? Lovingly, angrily, accusingly, melodiously?! How would we like to hear them used in this group? Can you always tell what someone is feeling when they say your name? How can you tell? Are you always right?

When is it OK to shout out someone's name? When is it not OK?

Notes

What's my name?

⑦

⏱ 10 mins

♀ ♀ ♀

☑ listening   ☑ concentration
☑ asking questions   ☑ observation
☑ memory
☑ taking turns

How to play Players write their name (or how they would like to be known) on a sticky label. They hide the label somewhere on their own clothes, for example in the top of their sock, in a pocket, under their collar or on the sole of their shoe.

Players try to find as many names as possible (within a time limit suitable for the size of the group) without touching anyone. They can only ask questions such as, 'Is it on the sole of your shoe?' or 'Can you show me underneath your right foot?' They either write down all the names that they find or try to remember them.

When the time limit is up everyone stands or sits in a circle. The game coordinator stands behind each person in turn and everyone tries to remember that person's name.

Adaptations

⑤

Throw a soft cushion around the group. Each person says her own name when she catches it. After everyone has had a turn, go round again. This time the rest of the group say the name of the person who catches the cushion.

Use a weighted or strangely shaped soft object so that everyone is likely to have some difficulty catching it – a fun way to even out the ability levels in the group.

Put name labels in a bowl. Each player picks out another player's name and tries to find that person in the group and present them with the label.

Make two sets of animal picture labels: one for players to wear and one to put in the bowl. Players pick an animal label from the bowl and find the matching picture worn by a group member.

Reflection What helps you to remember other people's names? What do you feel like when other people remember your name?

What sort of questions could you ask when you are getting to know someone?

Notes

Remember me

⑦

⏲ 10 mins

☑ listening
☑ memory
☑ taking turns
☑ concentration

How to play   Players sit in a circle. The first player says her own name. The second player says the first player's name and her own name, the third player says the first two names, and her own name, and so on around the group.

Adaptations   Names are said in time to rhythmic clapping to keep the momentum going.

⑤

Alternate players in the circle take turns to say their own name and the name of the person sitting on their right. This second player claps twice but does not speak. If anyone claps when they should be speaking or speaks when they should be clapping, the whole process changes direction.

Reflection   Is it harder or easier to remember names when you are concentrating on something else as well? Does this apply to other tasks? Does it depend on what the task is?

In later games sessions this could be linked with trying to remember calming strategies when we are feeling anxious. For example, if I'm trying to join in with a conversation and I am finding this difficult, it will be even harder if I get frustrated or anxious but easier if I remember to stay focused and calm.

Notes

Signs and signatures

⑦

⏱ 5 mins

♦ ♦ ♦

☑ listening
☑ memory
☑ taking turns
☑ concentration
☑ observation

☑ self-awareness
☑ awareness of
others
☑ non-verbal
communication

How to play   Players sit in a circle. The first player says his or her name accompanied by a movement/gesture (e.g. head movement, clapping, making sweeping gesture with both hands). The next person introduces the previous player (using their name and gesture) and then says their own name accompanied by their own gesture.

This is _____ and I am _____

Finish with everyone saying and gesturing their own name at the same time.

Adaptations   Players say their own name and think of a gesture but do not need to introduce anyone.

⑤

♀

Play the game standing up and include large movements such as jump back, shake leg, hop.

Teach the children specific signs, such as finger spelling for their initials or signs for different animals.

In smaller groups players can try and remember the names and gestures of as many previous players as possible (in a similar way to the game *Remember me* on p.64)

Reflection   If you had a different name, would you choose a different gesture? Do you think other people would link this gesture with your name?

Think of a family member or a friend. What gesture might they choose to go with their name? Would you choose a different gesture for them or the same one?

Does the gesture reflect your personality in some way? Talk about the differences and similarities in how you see yourself and how you think others see you.

Notes

Circle massage

⑤

🕐 5 mins

♀ ♀ ♀

♀

☑ self-awareness
☑ awareness of
    others
☑ taking turns

☑ empathy
☑ respect

Positive touch, such as this type of massage (performed by children on each other) can have a calming and relaxing effect. Incorporating a regular period of massage into a child's daily routine can help to increase concentration levels, decrease levels of agitation and aggression and help children to learn skills of empathy and tolerance.

How to play   Players sit in a circle with their backs to each other. Each player asks the person in front of her for permission to give them a massage. Players silently massage each other's back, neck and shoulders for two minutes. When the time is up everyone thanks the person who gave them a massage.

Adaptations   Players offer each other a back and shoulder massage in pairs. This helps the giver and receiver to really concentrate on what is happening. The receiver can ask their partner to alter the massage, for example by going more gently or more slowly.

Players take turns to close their eyes while their partner slowly draws a shape (circle, square, triangle) or writes a word on their palm with one finger. The person with their eyes closed has to guess the shape or word. They can ask for up to three repetitions if it is hard to guess. If they get it right they swap places.

One player sits facing away from the group. Everyone take turns to spell out their name in large letters on this person's back. If the first player guesses the name correctly the two swap places.

(See also the adapted version of *Pass the message* on p.90.)

Reflection   Talk about awareness of touch. Which is most sensitive to touch, your back or your finger tips? Are you aware of sensations all the time? For example do you notice your sleeves against your arms all day? Why is it important to be able to change the focus of our attention from one sensation to another or from one task or object to another? Is it possible to pay attention to two different senses or two different tasks at once?

Notes

Our story

⑤   ☑ listening   ☑ awareness of
⏲ 5 mins   ☑ concentration   others
👤 👤   ☑ self-awareness   ☑ self control
💬

This is a variation of a popular game called 'the old family coach'.

How to play   The game coordinator makes up a short story about the group, using each player's name at least three times. When a player hears his own name he stands up, turns round three times and takes a bow! When the game coordinator says, '*all the children*' or '*everyone*' the whole group stands up, turns round three times and takes a bow.

For example: 'The new classroom was ready at last and *all the children* waited excitedly in the playground on the first day of term. The head teacher asked *Edward* and *Jodie* to fetch the registers from the office. On the way inside they bumped into *Karen* and *Amarjeet* who had gone to fetch the school bell. *Sam* was allowed to ring the bell and he rang it so loudly that *Marcus* and *Sandeep* put their hands over their ears. Then *Edward* and *Michèle* led *everyone* into their new classroom...' and so on.

Adaptations   Use a response that requires only slight or no physical movement.

Use musical instruments for players to signal when they hear their name.

⑦

Base the story around an imaginary interaction which resulted in a misunderstanding that the children had to put right. This version of the activity is particularly effective if the story makes the children laugh.

Reflection   Saying someone's name is a good way to get their attention. What else is it OK to do when we want to say something to someone who doesn't seem to be listening? What is it *not* OK to do?

What do you feel if you don't hear something important?

When is it OK to laugh about something that goes wrong? When is it not OK?

Notes

Story-line

⑦
🕐 10 mins
👤 👤
💬💬💬

☑ listening
☑ memory
☑ respecting others
☑ research skills

☑ planning
☑ sequencing/
   story-telling

Players will need to do some research at home before this game can be played.

How to play   Players are given the task of researching their names in preparation for a subsequent session. Guide them with questions such as 'Do you know what your name means?' 'How was your name chosen?' 'How important is your name to you?' 'When you use your name, how do you use it?' 'Do you like other people to use your full name or a shortened version or do you have a favourite nickname?'

In the circle start by telling name stories in pairs. Each pair then takes turns to introduces their partner to the group and say one thing they remembered about that person's name story.

Adaptations   Research middle names.

In smaller groups take time to hear each person's name story in the circle.

Reflection   Do you know anyone else with the same name as you? Are they anything like you or are they very different? How many children have names that are a 'family' name, given to successive generations perhaps? How do they feel about that?

⑩   Do you associate some names with particular characteristics? Why might this happen?

Do you like to use a different name with your family and with your friends? If so, why?

Notes

Important names

⑦

🕐 5 mins

♦ ♦ ♦

💬

☑ listening
☑ self-awareness
☑ respecting others
☑ taking turns

☑ understanding
characteristics

I use a Tibetan bell for the adapted version of this game. Children ring it just once and say their name as the chime resonates around the room. It can add a wonderful sense of grandeur and dignity to the sound of each name.

How to play   Each person chooses a special word to describe herself, beginning with the first letter of her name (e.g. energetic Erin, happy Hilary). Stand in a circle and use a softball or beanbag to throw. On the first round the catcher says her own special name. On the second round the thrower calls out another player's special name as she throws the ball/ beanbag to her.

Adaptations   Players choose special names to reflect particular talents (not necessarily using the first letter of their name).

⑤   Use a small bell with a clapper. The first player carries the bell slowly across the circle to another player, trying not to let it ring. The person who receives the bell rings it loudly and says their special name (younger children can just say their first name). They then carry the bell across the circle to another player and so on until everyone has had a turn.

Reflection   Think about the enjoyment of saying and hearing your own name. How can you celebrate your name? Take time to reflect on the qualities in yourself that you really like. Why is self-respect important? How do we show self-respect and respect for others?

Notes

Party guests

⑨

🕐 10 mins

† † †

◯◯

☑ listening
☑ memory
☑ taking turns
☑ concentration

☑ self-awareness
☑ respecting others

How to play   Each member of the group thinks of a true fact that she would like other group members to know about her. This should be a personal statement about an ability, like or dislike. Players introduce themselves to each other in pairs and share their personal statements. All pairs then walk around the room together introducing their partners and responding to introductions from others. For example, 'This is Moira and she loves swimming,' 'Hello Moira, I'm Jan and this is Ryan. He's really good at drawing cartoons.'

Adaptation

⑩

Players invent something amazing to say about their partner, based on what is already known about his or her interests and personality. For example, 'This is Moira and she is the youngest person ever to swim the Channel.'

Reflection   Children don't normally introduce each other in such a formal way but when might such formal introductions be used? How else might we get to know facts about each other?

Notes

Additional notes: more ideas for warm-ups and ice-breakers

Reflections

9

Staying on track:
self-awareness and self-control

Puppets

⑤

🕐 5 mins

👤 👤 👤

🗨

☑ self-awareness
☑ self-control
☑ concentration
☑ cooperation

How to play   Players pretend to be puppets. They start in a standing position with their feet firmly on the ground, their arms stretched upwards and fingers spread out as though they are being held up by strings. They imagine that the strings are very slowly being loosened so that their body starts to drop down. Start with just the fingers, then hands, arms, head and upper body, finally bending slightly at the knees. The same movements are then performed in reverse until all players are standing upright again with arms stretched as high as they can. Do this several times at varying speeds.

Adaptation   In pairs take turns at being puppet and puppeteer. Without touching the
⑦   puppet the puppeteer pretends to pull strings to get different parts of the puppet to move in different directions and at different speeds. This works well if the puppet is lying down to start with and the puppeteer has to work out which strings to pull in order to get the puppet to stand up.

Reflection   How does your body move? What aspects of movements can you control (speed, direction, range). Think about the complicated sequence of movements needed to stand up or sit down. How do we learn how to do this? Talk about how children make mistakes and fall over when they are learning but as we get older we move without thinking about it. Can you tell when your muscles are relaxed and when they are tense? Do you ever think about your shoulders, your back, the backs of your knees?!

How did the puppet and the puppeteer cooperate? What did you each need to do? How easy or difficult was this? Which role did you enjoy the most?

Notes

Sleeping bear

⑤

🕐 10 mins

♦ ♦ ♦

☿

☑ self-awareness
☑ self-control
☑ listening

☑ tolerating
   frustration

How to play   The game coordinator chooses the first person to be the bear. This person sits on a chair in the middle of the circle or at the far end of the room, blind-folded. A bunch of keys is placed under the chair. The game coordinator chooses a player to creep up to the chair and steal the keys before the bear can point at him or her. If they manage to get the keys then he or she becomes the new bear.

Adaptation   Two players at a time cross the room from opposite ends. They both keep their eyes shut. One is the hunter and one is the bear. They must both move slowly and cautiously and listen carefully. The hunter tries to catch the bear and the bear tries to stay away from the hunter.

Reflection   Talk about self-control and self-awareness. Talk about the difference between listening with full attention and hearing noises without fully attending.

Notes

All birds fly

⑥

🕐 5 mins

👤 👤 👤

💬

☑ self-awareness
☑ self-control
☑ concentration
☑ observation

☑ tolerating
frustration

How to play   This is another version of 'Simon says'. The aim is for the caller to 'catch players out' by getting them to flap their arms at the wrong time. A chosen player starts the game by flapping his or her arms like a bird and saying 'all birds fly'. All other players in the group flap their arms in response. The caller then names a mixture of birds, animals and objects in random order, flapping his or her arms every time, e.g. 'eagles fly', 'sparrows fly', 'monkeys fly', 'chairs fly', 'crows fly'. The rest of the group should only flap their arms when a bird is called. If any player flaps when an animal or an object is called they have to stand still for the next two calls.

Each caller has ten turns before handing over to another caller.

Adaptations   The same game could be played with 'all fish swim'. The caller makes a swimming gesture with one hand.

The time for 'standing still' can be extended so that players experience waiting for longer periods.

Reflection   Was this easy or difficult? What helped you to control your responses? What were you feeling when you were waiting to join in again?

Notes

Sleeping giants

⑤
🕐 10 mins
🚶 🚶 🚶
💬

☑ self-awareness
☑ self-control
☑ waiting

How to play   Players pretend to be giants. They stamp around the room with heavy footsteps until the game coordinator gives a signal, such as ringing a small bell or raising one hand in the air. Then the giants lie down on the ground and close their eyes. The game coordinator walks quietly around the room to see if they are all 'asleep'. The coordinator can talk but must not touch the giants. If any giants are seen to move then they must sit up and keep looking for any others who are moving.

Adaptation   Use two different types of music – one loud with a heavy beat and one quiet and gentle. The giants move to the sound of the first and lie down when they hear the second; or they move more slowly to the gentle music and lie down when the music stops.

Reflection   How easy or difficult is it to stay still? What did the game coordinator do or say that caused you to move?

How easy or difficult is it to be active and to listen or watch for a signal from someone else?

When the giants were stamping around, did anyone bump into another giant? Why do you think this happened?

Notes

Pass a smile

⑤

🕐 5 mins

👤 👤

🗨

- ☑ self-awareness
- ☑ self-control
- ☑ taking turns
- ☑ concentration

- ☑ non-verbal
  communication

How to play   Players sit in a circle. Everyone tries to look very solemn. One player is chosen to start off a smile. He sends a smile to the person sitting next to him. This person smiles then 'zips' their lips in order to 'hold' the smile. He then turns to the next person and unzips the smile to pass it on! When the smile has been around the circle once, the group have a go at passing another smile but this time even more quickly.

Adaptations   'Throw' a smile across the circle. Everyone has to stay on the alert to catch it!

Pass a frown or a look of surprise.

Reflection   How does your body feel when you smile? What makes you smile? Can you tell the difference between a genuine smile and a pretend one or an 'unkind' smile? How can you tell the difference? Do you always know what expression you are showing on your face? For example, do you know when you are frowning or looking 'fed up'?

Notes

Giggle switch

⑤   ☑ self-awareness
🕐 5 mins   ☑ self-control
👤 👤 👤   ☑ taking turns
💬   ☑ eye-contact

It is important to be aware of any cultural differences in the appropriateness of different levels of eye-contact when playing this game.

How to play   Pairs sit facing each other. They choose who is A and who is B. They must keep eye-contact and try to keep a straight face. The game coordinator waits until everyone is quiet and then says 'giggle switch', at which point person A tries to make person B giggle in any way they can without touching them. At any time the coordinator can say 'giggle switch' again and the players have to swap roles.

Adaptations   Players lie down on the floor in a circle with heads nearly touching in the centre and feet facing towards the outside of the circle, their hands resting gently on their stomachs. The first person starts off by saying 'ha!', the second says 'ha ha!', the third says 'ha ha ha!', and so on, going as fast as possible until someone starts to laugh for real. Then everyone has to wait for silence before another player starts off a round of 'ho!'

This can also be played with each person lying with their head on someone else's stomach. The movement involved in saying 'ha!' can cause laughter before the round gets very far at all!

Reflection   How easy or difficult is it to keep eye-contact? When two people are talking to each other do they keep eye-contact all the time? Is eye-contact appropriate for some people/situations and not for others? What are some of the different 'messages' that we give when we vary the length of eye-contact or avoid it all together?

Talk about the importance of laughter. How do you feel when you have had a 'fit of the giggles'? Talk about the difference between 'laughing at someone' and 'laughing with someone'. Sometimes people laugh when they are anxious or embarrassed. Laughter can have very different qualities and can therefore cause us to feel quite differently too.

Notes

This and that

⑤

🕐 5 mins

↑ ↑ ↑

💬

☑ self-awareness
☑ self-control
☑ listening
☑ concentration

☑ tolerating
frustration

How to play   The game coordinator demonstrates simple movements for players to follow such as stand on one leg, touch your ear, wave, clap. When the instruction is 'do this' then players copy the movement. When the instruction is 'do that' no one is supposed to move. Anyone who moves by mistake must stand still for the next two instructions.

Adaptations   Instead of standing still when mistakes are made, players continue to join in but move to an inner circle. It is likely that all players will be in this circle before very long!

Play 'Simon says' while holding on to a parachute. Movements will be based on leg, head or whole body movements e.g. stand on one leg, nod your head, shake your shoulders, shake your foot.

Vary the speed at which the instructions are given.

Reflection   Talk about self-awareness and self-control. When we repeat something often enough we begin not to notice what we are doing. Why is this useful? When might it not be useful? What helps you to concentrate?

Notes

Melting snowman

⑤

🕐 5 mins

👤 👤 👤

💬

☑ self-awareness

☑ self-control

☑ relaxation skills

☑ imagination

☑ dramatic
awareness

How to play   Spread out around the room so that everyone has plenty of space in which to 'melt'. Players start by imagining that they are a newly built snowman. They stand very still with their arms by their sides. Each person makes all their muscles tense. Now they imagine the sun has come out and it is getting warmer. The snowmen start to 'melt' until they are pools of melted snow on the floor. Everyone lies very still, letting all their muscles go floppy. Now it starts to snow so that they can be built up into snowmen again. Melt once more. Then they are back to being themselves again. Ask them to stand up tall and shake their arms, hands and legs as if they are shaking the snow off.

Adaptations   Alternate between being a rag doll and a wooden or metal toy.

Use different music to indicate when it is time to melt and when it is time to be a snowman.

Reflection   What does it feel like to be tense and what does it feel like to be very relaxed? Notice the difference between being very tense as a snowman and feeling strong without feeling excessive tension. Why is it important for our bodies to be relaxed sometimes? Is there such a thing as useful tension? When do we need to be tense? Are there times when you have tension in your body that doesn't need to be there?

Notes

Run-around

⑤
🕐 5 mins
👤 👤
💬

☑ self-awareness
☑ awareness of
    others
☑ taking turns

☑ cooperation
☑ concentration

How to play   One person is chosen to start the game off (player A). The rest of the players stand in a close circle, facing the centre. Player A walks slowly around the outside of the circle and taps someone on the shoulder. That person and player A then run in opposite directions around the outside of the circle to see who can get back to the space first. The player left out of the circle then walks slowly around the outside and chooses another person by tapping them on the shoulder.

Adaptation   Players hop in opposite directions to get to the available space.

Reflection   What do you feel like if you are on the outside of a group? How can you help others to join a group that you are already in? What do you do when you want to join a group who are already playing or working together? What could you say to the group? When is it easy to join a group? When might it be difficult?

Notes

Adverts

⑩
🕐 50 mins
† † †
♀♀♀

☑ self-awareness
☑ creative thinking
☑ cooperation

☑ understanding
   characteristics

This game helps children to recognize and explore some of the skills and attributes that they have in relation to different aspects of their lives.

How to play   Each player chooses a 'role' from a provided list. This could be a role that they actually play in life or one they would like to play. This works best if at least three people choose each role. Players are then grouped together according to their choices and cooperate to design a joint poster or TV advert for themselves in this particular role, highlighting skills and attributes. Volunteers share their posters in the circle.

Possible roles might be: sports ace, computer expert, brother/sister, son/daughter, friend, artist, science whiz kid, inventor, builder.

Adaptations   Design 'your class needs you' posters highlighting attributes and skills needed for successful group work.

Design individual adverts.

Reflection   Everyone has valuable skills and attributes. What skill or attribute are you most proud of? What is the difference between boasting and being proud about something? (Boasting and 'putting others down' can be how some children respond when their own feelings of self-worth are low.)

How are your skills valuable to others? Do you have a skill that you can teach to others in this group?

Notes

Emotion sensations

⑧

⏱ 60 mins

� ♦ ♦ ♦

♡

☑ self-awareness
☑ understanding feelings
☑ concentration

☑ observation
☑ creative thinking

This requires some preparation by the game coordinator beforehand.

How to play   Divide the group into two halves. Groups A and B then work in different rooms or in different parts of the same room but must not look at what the other group is doing. Within each group players work in pairs or threes to draw round each other's body outline on large pieces of paper. Each player uses pictures from comics, catalogues, magazines etc. to 'clothe' their body outline with shapes and colours or objects to represent how his or her body feels when they experience a particular emotion, such as nervousness.

Group A try to guess who each of the pictures belong to in group B and vice versa.

Adaptations   Once clothed, add words, headlines and catchphrases to represent useful and not useful aspects of different emotions, for example anger.

⑩   Players each pick an emotion card from a selection provided by the game coordinator and make their body pictures according to the chosen emotion. Everyone tries to guess the emotion portrayed.

Make a joint picture for one emotion, each player adding a different physical symptom.

Reflection   When you look at all the figures can you see anything that any of them have in common? What are the main differences?

When might a feeling of nervousness be useful? What other feelings might cause similar sensations in your body? (e.g. a knotted stomach could be excitement, clenched fists could be a linked with determination). How does your body feel different when you are happy? What about when you are confident? If you are anxious and you change the way your body feels (e.g. by smiling and relaxing your muscles) do you start to feel a different emotion?

Notes

Additional notes: more ideas for exploring self-awareness and self-control

Reflections

Tuning in:
exploring effective listening
and effective observation

Sound tracking

⑤
🕐 10 mins
♂ ♀
💬

☑ listening
☑ deduction
☑ self-control
☑ concentration

How to play The group sit silently in the centre of a darkened room with their eyes closed. The game coordinator hides a clock in the room. Each player tries to locate the clock through listening only. The player who is the most accurate in their description of where the clock is (e.g. next to the door, on top of the bookcase) takes the next turn to hide the clock.

Adaptations The clock is hidden before players enter the room.

Blindfolded players all point in the direction of the clock at the same time. The game coordinator decides who is the most accurate.

Two clocks are placed in different locations and players have to find both of them.

Players sit with their eyes closed and try to identify as many different sounds as possible, e.g. a ticking clock, the sound of breathing, traffic noises outside, the rain on the window.

Reflection How easy or difficult is it to sit really still and listen? What makes it easier? What makes it harder? Did you hear noises that you hadn't noticed before? When is it useful to be able to choose what we listen to and ignore all the other sounds around us?

What sounds do you like to listen to? What sounds in the environment don't you like?

Notes

Calling cards

⑤   ☑ listening   ☑ volume of speech
⏱ 5 mins   ☑ memory
👤 👤 👤   ☑ concentration
💬   ☑ cooperation

How to play   Players select one card each from a pile of cards showing common objects that go together such as a card showing a toothbrush and a card showing toothpaste, or a letter and a postbox. Players stand in a circle and everyone calls out what is on their card at the same time. The aim is for each person to find their 'partner'.

Adaptations   Players find their opposite e.g. up/down; big/little; hot/cold.

Players find two others in the same category e.g. happy, excited, elated.

Half the group have cards with questions on such as 'why is the girl laughing?' The other half of the group have 'because' cards e.g. 'because her friend has told her a funny joke.'

Reflection   What is the difference between hearing and listening? How do you know when someone has *listened* to what you have said? How do you *show* that you are listening? What sort of things do people say to indicate that they are listening?

Notes

Pass the message

⑤
🕐 10 mins
🚹 🚹 🚹
💬💬

☑ listening
☑ observation
☑ reflecting on behaviour

☑ concentration
☑ taking turns
☑ tolerating frustration

How to play
Players are seated in a circle. Player One whispers a short sentence to the next person in the circle, who whispers it to the next person and so on until it gets back to Player One again. The final sentence heard is then compared to the original version.

Adaptations
Player One draws a simple shape or picture with one finger on the back of Player Two who has to pass it on around the circle.

Player One draws a simple picture on a piece of paper then shows it briefly to Player Two who has to draw it from memory before showing the new version to Player Three and so on.

Reflection
Compare the different versions of the pictures or the spoken sentences. Is it easy or difficult to remember the details of what we see and hear? Talk about how things we say and do can be remembered inaccurately. What should we do if we think someone has misunderstood us or we don't really understand what someone else has said?

When is it OK for something that you have said to be repeated to other people? When is it not OK?

Notes

Keep it going

⑦
🕐 10 mins
👤 👤
💬

- ☑ observation
- ☑ memory
- ☑ taking turns
- ☑ concentration
- ☑ non-verbal communication
- ☑ sequencing

How to play   Players sit or stand behind each other in a line. The first player taps the second player on the shoulder. This person turns to face the first player who then mimes a short sequence such as planting a seed in a pot and watering it, or cutting a slice of bread and spreading butter on it. The second player has to remember the sequence to show to the third player and so on. The final player tries to guess what the first player was actually miming.

Adaptations   The sequence can be made longer and more complicated or simplified to include just two parts.

Players work in pairs and pass on sequences of gestures which involve two people cooperating e.g. folding a large sheet together.

Reflection   Did the sequence change as it was passed around the group? Why did this happen? Do you use gesture when you talk? Why is it helpful to notice people's body language?

Notes

'Eye' spy

⑦
🕐 10 mins
👤 👤 👤
💬💬💬

☑ observation   ☑ trust
☑ respecting others
☑ taking turns
☑ eye-contact

How to play   Players walk around the room and meet each other. Each time they meet up with someone they stay and look at each other's eyes for at least 30 seconds, taking turns to describe exactly what the other person's eyes look like – not just the main colour but as many other details as possible.

Adaptations   Children use mirrors to draw their own eyes and colour them in with as much detail as possible. The group tries to guess the owners of the drawings.

Reflection   Why is eye contact important when we communicate with each other? What do you like about your eyes? When you walk do you look down at the ground most of the time or do you look around you? What messages do our eyes give to others?

Notes

Circle move

⑤   ☑ observation   ☑ eye-contact
⏱ 5 mins   ☑ taking turns
♦ ♦ ♦   ☑ concentration
💬   ☑ self-awareness

How to play   Players sit in a circle. One person starts off a movement such as a shoulder shake. Each player copies this in turn until everyone is making the same movement. Then everyone stops in turn until the circle is still. The person sitting to the left of the first player then starts a different movement and sends this around the group in the same way. Do this as many times as feels comfortable, varying the speed.

Adaptations   Two players sitting on opposite sides of the circle start off two different movements at the same time and send them in the same direction or in opposite directions.

Players 'throw' the movement to each other across the circle by gaining eye contact with another player.

Reflection   Sometimes even small movements or changes in body posture can show other people how we are feeling or can add extra emphasis to what we are saying. How many emotions can you show just by moving your shoulders? What about when you move your forehead/eyebrows?

Notes

All change

⑥
🕐 5 mins
🚶 🚶 🚶
🗨

☑ observation
☑ memory
☑ awareness of
    others

How to play
One player leaves the room. Someone in the group changes something about herself (e.g. removes her shoes, puts on a jumper, or ties her hair back). The observer returns and tries to guess who has changed and what they have changed.

Adaptation
Two players leave the room. Three people change something physically or change places and the two players have to say what the changes are.

Reflection
Talk about observation skills and looking with full awareness as opposed to just 'glancing' at something. Why do we need to be selective in what we pay attention to at any one time?

Notes

Five and a joker

⑦

⏲ 10 mins

☑ observation
☑ memory
☑ concentration
☑ asking questions

☑ awareness of others

How to play Pairs of players take turns to sit in the centre of the group. They have an allotted time to study each other carefully, noting hair colour, eye colour, clothes etc. They then turn and sit back to back. The rest of the group call out questions such as, 'What colour are Becky's socks?' The players in the centre score one point for every correct answer. At any time during their turn a player can use a 'joker' before answering. This will give them five points if they are correct. The round continues until both players in the centre have 10 points.

Adaptations The length of time allocated for observation is increased or decreased.

The same set of questions is used for each pair.

Three players sit in the centre and answer questions about each other.

Reflection Talk about similarities and differences. What would the world be like if we all dressed in exactly the same way? What would be good about that? What would not be good about that?

Notes

Guess how!

⑦
🕐 10 mins
🚶 🚶 🚶
💬

☑ listening
☑ concentration
☑ observation
☑ self-awareness

☑ deduction

How to play Two players leave the room while everyone else decides what 'angry position' or 'calm position' they should take up on their return. For anger this might be something like 'sitting on the floor, facing away from each other with arms and legs folded'. The two players return and try to work out how they should be sitting or standing according to how loudly or quietly the rest of the group are clapping. The closer they get to the target position, the louder everyone else claps.

Adaptation The two players who left the room return and 'arrange' two other players in pre-chosen positions.

Reflection Sometimes we get feedback from others about whether or not we're succeeding in a task or we're 'on the right track' but sometimes we have to rely on our own self-awareness. Talk about being realistic in self-awareness. How do you know when you are doing something well? How do you know when you are tense or when you are relaxed? How do you know when you need to do something in a different way?

Notes

Additional notes: more ideas for exploring effective listening and effective observation

Reflections

11

More than just talking: communication skills

Silent greetings

⑤
🕐 10 mins
👤 👤 👤
🗨

- ☑ greetings
- ☑ ending an interaction
- ☑ non-verbal communication

- ☑ flexibility in communication
- ☑ awareness of proximity to others
- ☑ observation

This game requires plenty of space for players to move around freely.

How to play Everyone walks slowly around the room, silently greeting each other in a friendly way. For example, a little wave, a long slow wave, offering 'high five', smiling, making eye-contact, having a short 'conversation' between hands. The game coordinator may need to demonstrate a few ideas first. There should be no physical contact during this. The aim is to see how many different ways players can greet each other successfully.

Adaptations Play a variety of music (e.g. culturally specific music, lively music, slow, gentle music) while players walk around the room and greet each other in ways that match the different rhythms and themes.

Players meet and greet each other. After a short silent 'conversation' they say goodbye to each other non-verbally.

Reflection Did you learn a new greeting or get a new idea and then try it out on someone else? Did some ways of greeting seem easier than others? What was the most fun/natural/relaxed way to greet others? Which one felt most like 'you'? Did you change your greetings to match other people or did pairs sometimes greet each other in completely different ways? How did that feel?

What are some of the signs that you could look out for to show you that people are thinking about you, or welcoming you into a group, even if they don't say anything (e.g. 'thumbs up', smile)? How might this help you if you are feeling anxious? Can you think of a time when you would be able to give this type of reassurance to someone else?

How close do we stand to the other person when we greet each other?

What are some of the other ways that people greet each other? (e.g. shaking hands, a back slap, a hug).

What sort of things can you say to end a conversation? How do you know when a conversation is coming to an end?

Notes

Beginnings and endings

⑦
🕐 20 mins

☑ beginning an
   interaction
☑ ending an
   interaction
☑ listening

☑ asking questions
☑ maintaining a topic
☑ taking turns

How to play   Players sit in a circle and throw a bean bag or soft ball to each other. The catcher thinks of a phrase or question that could be used to start off an interaction such as 'Did you stay for football practice last night?', 'Can I play too?' or 'I'm not sure how to do this. Can you help me please?' If a player is unable to think of something then they can choose from two suggestions offered by the game coordinator or offered by the rest of the group.

When everyone has had a turn players then think of ways to end an interaction such as 'Bye. See you tomorrow', or 'Thanks for your help'.

Adaptations   The beginnings and endings are written on cards and placed in two piles. Pairs of players pick one from each pile. They have five minutes to prepare a conversation that makes use of the beginning and ending written on the cards. Pairs then demonstrate their conversation to the whole group.

Pairs choose a card from each pile and must make up a spontaneous conversation using both cards within 60 seconds.

Reflection   Did pairs stay on the same topic for their conversation?

What helps you to stay on the topic?

What happens if one person in the conversation suddenly changes the topic?

Notes

Questions and answers

⑩
🕑 10 mins

☑ asking/answering questions
☑ deduction
☑ listening

☑ memory
☑ taking turns
☑ respecting others

How to play   Everyone in the group writes the name of a famous person on a piece of paper (or these could be prepared beforehand by the game coordinator). The papers are then shuffled and each person takes one without looking at it. This is taped to his or her back by the game coordinator. Players form a circle and take turns to stand in the middle, turning around slowly so that everyone can read the label. The player in the centre can ask up to twenty questions to find out the identity of the famous person. The other players can only answer 'yes' or 'no'.

Adaptations   Use animal pictures or characters from a book with which the players are all familiar.

Allow more descriptive answers than just 'yes' or 'no'.

Reflection   How easy or difficult was it to think up questions?

How did you use the answers to each question to help you to decide on the next question?

In order to know someone well we need to know lots of different things about them. What sort of things could we ask? Think about personality, opinions, likes and dislikes etc.

Notes

Magic threes

⑦

⏱ 10 mins

☑ asking/answering questions

☑ giving personal information

☑ listening

☑ memory

☑ taking turns

☑ respecting others

How to play   Players have three minutes to walk around the room and introduce themselves to three other people. Each player asks three people three questions. For younger children this could be full name, something you hate and something you like. For older children the questions could be what is your greatest achievement, your best birthday and your most treasured possession? Or one thing that makes you angry, one thing you do to 'chill out' and one thing you want to achieve.

When the time is up, everyone sits in a circle and recounts as much information about as many other players as possible.

Adaptations   Pairs share the information and then introduce each other to the rest of the group.

Players divide into groups of three or four and try to find three things that they all have in common. One person from each small group tells the whole group what these three things were.

Reflection   What type of question is likely to produce a limited amount of information? What type of question encourages people to give more detailed information? How difficult or easy was it to remember what you heard? What would make it easier/harder to remember facts about other people? Why is it important to remember what people tell us about themselves? What does it feel like when someone remembers something important about you? What does it feel like when people get the facts wrong?

Is it better to ask three questions all at once or to ask them one at a time? How long can you comfortably wait in order to give the other person time to think of their answer?

What does it feel like to know that you have things in common with other people? Was it difficult or easy to find things in common?

Notes

Personal interviews

⑦
🕐 10 mins
♦ ♦ ♦
👄👄👄

☑ asking/answering questions
☑ encouraging/ reinforcing others
☑ trust

☑ listening
☑ taking turns
☑ giving personal information

How to play
Drape a chair with a brightly coloured blanket or cloth. Players take turns to sit in the chair and are interviewed by the rest of the group. Questions can be about their likes and dislikes, wishes, holidays, favourite books, pet hates, etc. or they can be interviewed about a particular interest they have. There is an allocated time limit for each interview. Reassure everyone that they will have a turn at being interviewed at another time if they want to.

Adaptations
Use two chairs, one for the person being interviewed and one for volunteer interviewers who can come and sit in the chair and ask one question before returning to their place in the audience.

The interviewee takes on the role of a famous person or a character in a book.

Reflection
How does it feel to have the chance to talk about yourself? How does 'being interviewed' compare to having a conversation with someone? Talk about taking turns in conversations and asking questions to show a genuine interest in the other person. What does it feel like when a friend asks you questions about yourself?

How do you encourage someone to carry on talking or to give you more details about something?

How do you show that you are thinking about what to say? What happens if someone asks a lot of questions without giving the interviewee time to answer?

Notes

Surprise stories

⑦

⏱ 15 mins

☑ sequencing ideas   ☑ taking turns
☑ imagination
☑ maintaining a topic
☑ listening

How to play   A cloth bag full of interesting objects is passed around the group. The first player takes an object without looking inside the bag. He must then start off a story based on that object. The bag then passes to player B who takes an object and must weave that into the story as quickly as possible. The story continues until all objects have been used.

Adaptations   Themed objects are placed in the bag, such as farm animals, a farmer and a tractor or small objects that might be taken on holiday.

Each player takes three objects and makes up a whole story within a strict time limit.

Volunteers tell stories based on one or more objects from the bag.

Reflection   Talk about working in a group to deal with the unexpected. —

What does it feel like when someone changes the story that you had in your mind?

Talk about being spontaneous. Often it is good to plan ahead but sometimes we can over-plan things and get anxious about something long before it ever happens.

Notes

Tell me my story

⑨
🕐 10 mins
� �
♡♡♡

☑ sequencing ideas   ☑ imagination
☑ maintaining a topic
☑ empathy
☑ listening

How to play   The game coordinator provides a title which includes a player's name such as:

Marcus the bold

Amazing Craig

Javed's dream day out

Katie's greatest adventure

The player in question starts off the story. The rest of the group continue around the circle, saying one sentence each. This could be a completely imaginary story or could relate to something that everyone knows really happened.

Adaptations   Players think up their own title for their stories.

Players choose titles from a selection of three or four.

Reflection   Was this difficult, exciting, funny, easy? Did the group come up with some things that truly reflected each person's personality/likes and dislikes?

How did it feel to listen to a story about yourself?

Notes

Conversation drawings

⑦

🕐 15 mins

♦ ♦ ♦

♀

☑ joining in/starting a conversation

☑ imagination

☑ self-awareness

☑ awareness of others

☑ taking turns

☑ non-verbal communication

How to play   Players work in pairs to construct a conversation through drawing, making marks and shapes with paint or crayons on the same piece of paper. Each player uses one colour and takes turns to draw their part of the conversation. Players must keep to their own half of the paper.

Adaptations   Players construct 'happy' conversations.

Players construct angry conversations or 'I'm worried' conversations. Finish with a resolution and a calming down for these two interactions.

Players work in groups of three.

Two pairs of players construct their own conversation at opposite ends of a large piece of paper. After one or two minutes they then join up with each other to share a conversation between all four of them.

Spread a roll of plain wallpaper across a large space (the school playground is ideal for this) so that players can move around and have 'art conversations' with as many different people as possible, joining groups, starting new groups or talking to just one other person at a time.

Reflection   What skills do you have that help you to join conversations and to start new conversations? What happens if people talk at the same time as each other? What happens if lots of people want to join the same conversation?

Notes

Hand talk

⑨
🕐 10 mins
♦ ♦ ♦
♡

☑ non-verbal communication
☑ self-awareness

☑ awareness of others
☑ imagination

Players need to stand in a large enough space so that they have room to move their arms and hands without touching anyone else.

How to play   The game coordinator instructs players to shake their arms and then to move their hands loosely, keeping them at shoulder level. When the game coordinator says 'freeze' everyone drops one hand and holds the other hand still. They then think about what name they would give to this gesture e.g. 'inquisitive', 'ferocious', 'sad' or 'puzzled'. Each person changes their hand posture very slightly. What name would they give to this new gesture? Players invent a 'hand dance' changing from one gesture to its opposite and back again.

Adaptations   Shake your whole body or just let yourself move freely. Freeze. Give this posture a name. Change the way you are standing slightly. What would you call this posture?

Limit the possibilities to just a few such as happy, sad and angry.

Reflection   Talk about how even subtle changes in body language can make a big difference to how we feel and to how other people *think* we feel. Can you think of postures that look nearly the same but mean something very different?

Notes

Pass the shell

⑦
🕐 5 mins
† † †
◯◯

☑ giving and
   receiving praise
☑ listening
☑ trust

☑ empathy
☑ taking turns

How to play   Use a large shell or a beautiful/unusual object of some sort. Pass the shell around the group. Whoever is holding it praises someone else and passes them the shell. This is best done in sequence around the circle to start with until you feel that children can praise each other in random order and not leave anyone out.

Adaptations   Each player has a piece of paper and writes their name at the bottom. The papers are passed around the group for everyone to write something positive about the person named on the paper. The paper is folded over after each comment has been added so that no one sees what anyone else has written. The paper is then returned to the original player to read silently.

Everyone has a piece of paper pinned to their back for others to write praises on.

Reflection   What does it feel like to give and receive praise? How many different ways can we praise each other? What would you most like to be praised for? What do you think your mother/brother/best friend would most like to be praised for? Is there anything you *don't* like to be praised for?

Notes

Guess the voice

⑦
🕐 10 mins
🚹🚹🚹
🗨

☑ awareness of voice patterns
☑ listening
☑ deduction
☑ memory
☑ taking turns
☑ concentration

How to play

Players stand or sit in a circle. Each player invents a unique vocal call, for example a combination of vowels with different intonation patterns or a hum or a whistle. The whole group listens to each call in turn as the players say their first name and then their chosen sound.

One person stands in the centre of the circle with a blindfold on. The game coordinator silently chooses someone to make their call. The person in the centre tries to name the caller. If they get it right they can have a second turn.

Each person has a maximum of two turns before the coordinator chooses another person to sit in the centre.

Adaptations

⑤

Callers recite one line of a well-known song or a pre-chosen phrase that all the players are able to say/remember.

The player in the centre asks 'who is there?' and those in the circle take turns to answer 'me', making the guessing harder.

Two people stand in the centre and can confer about the name of the caller.

The person who was last in the centre can choose the next caller.

Everyone changes seats before the caller is chosen.

The players are split into pairs to practise their calls. One person from each pair then stands in the centre of the circle and is blindfolded. On a signal their partners make their chosen calls. The players who are blindfolded have to carefully move around the circle until they find their partner.

Reflection

How do we recognize individual voices? What makes our voices different? What might happen if we all sounded exactly the same? What words can we use to describe different voices? (for example deep, gruff, loud, soft, like chocolate). Keep these descriptions very general, rather than specific to individual players.

Does your voice change according to how you are feeling?

Notes

Instructors

⑦

🕐 10 mins

👤 👤 👤

💬💬💬

☑ giving instructions
☑ listening
☑ self-awareness

☑ awareness of
others
☑ concentration

How to play
Working in pairs, players take turns to explain to their partner how to draw an object such as a car, a tree or a house. The person who is drawing must follow the instructions as accurately as possible even if the end result doesn't look like the intended object. Players swap roles after a set time period.

Adaptation
Pairs sit opposite each other with a visual barrier between them (e.g. a piece of card or an open book) so that they cannot see each other's drawings. The game coordinator provides simple line drawings for instructors to describe to their partners.

Reflection
What should you do if you are uncertain about an instruction that you have been given? What helps you to give clear instructions?

Notes

Additional notes: more ideas for communication skills games

Reflections

12

You and me: exploring feelings and developing empathy

Musical drawings

⑦
🕐 **20 mins**
🧍 🧍 🧍
💬

☑ **understanding feelings**
☑ **self-awareness**
☑ **listening**

☑ **imagination**

How to play   The game coordinator plays a variety of music and the group draws whatever comes to mind while listening to the different rhythms and moods.

Adaptation   Players bring in their own selections of music and talk about how they feel when they listen to it.

Reflection   Talk about how music can affect our mood. Is there a piece of music that always makes you feel sad or always makes you feel happy?

Notes

Freeze frame

⑤
🕐 5 mins
🔆 🔆 🔆
💬

☑ understanding feelings
☑ self-awareness

☑ non-verbal communication
☑ imagination

How to play
The game coordinator suggests different emotions and all members of the group try to show these emotions in any non-verbal way they like, for example as an animal, as a movement, by facial expression or the way they walk. The coordinator shouts 'freeze' and everyone 'holds' the pose and feels what it's like for a few seconds.

Shake that feeling out of the body (shake arms, hands, legs). Then try a different emotion. Finish with at least two positive emotions.

Adaptation
Act out actions and feelings together randomly e.g. doing the ironing sadly, eating a sandwich angrily.

Reflection
Sometimes we can be saying one thing and feeling something completely different. Does our body language sometimes 'give the game away'? If someone tells you they are angry but they are smiling would you believe their words or their facial expression?

How do you usually show that you are angry? How do you usually show that you are happy or sad?

Notes

Ladder of feelings

⑦
🕓 30 mins
♦ ♦ ♦
🗨🗨🗨

☑ understanding feelings
☑ empathy
☑ cooperation

☑ categorization
☑ negotiation
☑ trust

This game is about recognizing other people's feelings and noting similarities in feelings. It also helps children to recognize different degrees of emotion. You will need to make enough large wall charts for the number of groups playing plus one extra. Each chart should have four giant ladders drawn on it – one for each emotional theme.

How to play
Groups are given a time limit in which to think of as many feeling words as possible within the four themes of anger, fear, sadness and joy. Each word is written on separate cards. Players in each group then decide between themselves where each emotion word should be placed on the ladders. For example 'furious' and 'annoyed' would be placed on the anger ladder but annoyed would be near the bottom of the ladder and furious would be higher up. Groups then combine to negotiate making a final wall chart to show all the emotions in an agreed order.

Adaptation
Mark out a long line on the floor to indicate a scale of one to ten. Groups of children choose a category and then each pick one of the emotion words from that category. They then arrange themselves in order of intensity along the line.

Reflection
Were there any disagreements about levels of emotions? Do some people experience emotions near the top of the ladders a lot of the time? How can we recognize different levels of similar emotions in ourselves and in others? Do we sometimes have a high intensity emotion for low intensity situations?

Notes

Hands up!

⑦
🕐 5 mins
👤 👤 👤
🗨

☑ understanding
   feelings
☑ self-awareness
☑ imagination

☑ non-verbal
   communication

This game can be based on any emotion that has different levels, e.g. degrees of happiness or anxiety. Players need to stand in a large enough space so that they have room to move their arms and hands without touching anyone else.

How to play   Demonstrate how we can move our arms freely in the air and at the same time shake our hands loosely. When all players are moving freely the game coordinator calls out a word that reflects a degree of anger (e.g. annoyed, frustrated, furious, cross). Players begin an angry conversation between their two hands. After 30 seconds the coordinator calls 'hands up'. Players raise their hands above their heads and stretch as high as they can go. The coordinator then calls another anger word and players drop their arms down and act out another conversation between their hands until the coordinator calls 'hands up' again. Continue for at least four levels of anger then finish with a calm conversation. Instead of 'hands up' at the end, the coordinator calls 'hand shake'. Players shake hands with themselves!

Adaptation   Invent a 'hand dance' changing from calm to angry and back again. In small groups players can take turns to demonstrate their hand dance or to teach it to the rest of the group.

Reflection   Talk about any physical tension evident during the game. Are there times when our hands show how we are feeling? If our hands are tense does anything happen to the rest of our body?

Talk about how even small changes in body tension and posture (e.g. unclenching your jaw or relaxing your hands) can make a big difference to how we feel and to how other people *think* we feel. Can you think of postures that look nearly the same but mean something very different?

How do you stand or sit when you are feeling angry? How do other people know when you are feeling angry? What is the smallest thing that you need to do or to say for other people to know how you are feeling?

Notes

Face masks

⑥
🕐 5 mins
👤 👤 👤
🗨

☑ understanding feelings
☑ self-awareness
☑ imagination

☑ non-verbal communication
☑ taking turns
☑ observation

How to play Players sit in a circle. The first player 'pulls a face' to show a strong emotion, then 'removes' the face with their hands as if it were a mask and passes it to the player on their left. This player 'puts on' the mask, copying the expression as accurately as possible. The second player then changes the expression and passes it on to the next person and so on around the circle.

Adaptations Introduce a limited number of options to pass around the circle e.g. happy,
⑤ sad and angry. Everyone practises these before the game starts.

⑦ Limit the part of the mask that can be altered e.g. only the eyes and eyebrows, or just the mouth.

Reflection Which masks did players think they were putting on? What emotions did players pass to others? Did these match up? Is it possible to show an emotion with just one part of the face? Were there different degrees of any similar emotions passed around? How do we show different degrees of emotion (e.g. by facial expression, posture, actions)?

Talk about how we can have different levels of the same feeling in different situations – like having a volume control or an intensity control – for example, we could be slightly frustrated when we make a mistake and furious when someone accuses us of something that we didn't do.

When might it be OK to 'mask' our feelings? When might this have a positive effect on someone else?

Notes

Follow my walk

⑦
🕐 10 mins
👤 👤 👤
💬💬

☑ empathy
☑ giving and
   accepting
   compliments

☑ trust
☑ self-awareness
☑ observation

How to play   Players stand in circle. A volunteer walks across the circle several times. The group members give positive comments about the way that the volunteer walked. For example, 'You held your head up; you looked well balanced; you smiled; your shoulders were relaxed.' Then everyone tries to walk in exactly the same way to really feel what it is like to walk like this person.

Have as many volunteers as possible and reassure everyone that they will get a go at another time if they want to.

Adaptations   Imagine a character role and try to walk as you think they would walk e.g. the strongest person in the world, an old person, someone who has just been told some good news.

Walk in different ways to reflect different emotions.

In pairs try and exactly mirror how your partner walks across the room.

Reflection   How does our walk express how we feel about ourselves? What parameters can be changed? (e.g. walking with light/heavy footsteps; large strides/small steps; slowly/quickly; with a 'bounce'; arms swinging/arms stiff).

Discuss similarities and differences in the way that people walk. Think about 'sameness' and differences in such things as looks, actions, likes and dislikes. What would the world be like if we all talked and moved in exactly the same way? Why would that be difficult? And *then* what would happen? How does it feel to 'walk in someone else's shoes'? How does it feel when someone else really tries to feel what it is like to be you?

Notes

If we were animals

⑤
🕐 10 mins
👤 👤 👤
💬

☑ empathy
☑ non-verbal
   communication

☑ understanding
   opposites
☑ imagination
☑ self-awareness

This game requires a large space for players to be able to move around freely.

How to play Take some time to brainstorm the characteristics that might be associated with different animals. For example, a cat could be calm, adventurous, agile and so on.

Each player silently chooses an animal from the list that somehow shows something about their own character. Divide the group into two. Half the group imagine becoming their chosen animal for a short while – moving around the room, greeting other animals and finding out their 'character'. The other half of the group sit and watch. Those who are watching can get up at any time and tap an animal on the shoulder to guess its identity. If the guess is correct that animal joins the observers. Keep going until all the animals have been guessed. The groups then swap over.

Adaptations The game coordinator chooses one of the animals from the above game. Everyone in the group tries to act like that animal for 30 seconds. The person who originally chose the animal (in the first game) can give 'directions' e.g. 'I'm a flamingo and I move like this. I speak like this. I don't like…but I do like… When I meet other flamingos I…' There is no 'correct' way to explore being this animal – for example, it doesn't matter if the person giving directions says, 'I'm a flamingo and I like to eat chocolate'!

Everyone will need a turn at directing others in how to be their animal so it is best to do this version of the game with small groups or in pairs.

Everyone chooses a completely different animal, perhaps one who has the opposite characteristic to the first one chosen. For example, if a player chose a noisy animal they could try being a quiet one, fast/slow, big/small etc.

All players go back to being the original animals and stand or sit in a circle to introduce themselves to the group and say one good thing about being this animal (e.g. I am a leopard and I can run very fast). Finish by 'stepping out' of the chosen animals. Everyone stretches and shakes their arms and legs and goes back to being themselves again.

Reflection   What did it feel like to be the animal that you chose? How are you like that animal? Did you find out anything new about anyone else?

Do you think you are sometimes like the first animal and sometimes like the second one? How does that feel? Talk about how the we can have different levels of the same feeling or characteristic in different situations – like having a volume control or an intensity control – for example, we could be energetic one minute and very sleepy the next; or happy and then suddenly sad; timid in one situation and very brave in another. (see *Face masks*, p.118).

How did it feel to be like someone else (their chosen animal)? Was it easy or difficult? Are you ever like that yourself?

Notes

Feel it, do it

⑦
🕐 5 mins
🚶 🚶 🚶
💬

☑ empathy
☑ understanding feelings
☑ self-awareness

☑ taking turns
☑ observation

How to play   Players stand in a circle facing each other. Volunteers take turns to take one step into the circle and show with their whole body the way that they are feeling today. Then they say their name (in a way that also reflects the emotion) and step back. The whole group steps forward and reflects back the action and the original person's name. Everyone steps back. The next volunteer steps forward. Players do not need to name the emotions.

Adaptations   Players start by crouching down low. Volunteers 'pop' up (like popcorn!) and then crouch down again when they have shown their feeling and said their name. The whole group 'pops' up to reflect the feeling and then crouches down to wait for the next volunteer.

⑤   The game coordinator suggests a limited number of emotions such as happy, sad and angry. Volunteers 'pop' up to show one of these emotions and everyone else guesses which emotion that person was showing.

Reflection   Do you ever have feelings that you don't understand or don't know why you feel that way? Do people show the same emotions in different ways? Do you ever feel happy or sad or angry just because someone else is feeling like that?

Notes

Mirror talking

⑤   ☑ empathy   ☑ trust
🕐 5 mins   ☑ self-awareness   ☑ observation
🕴 🕴 🕴   ☑ non-verbal
💬   communication

How to play   Players sit opposite each other in pairs and take turns to mirror each other's hand movements as closely as possible.

Adaptations   Use music to evoke different moods for the hand movements.

Give a theme beforehand.

Extend to arm movements or whole body movements.

Reflection   How easy or difficult was this? What skills are needed in order to follow someone else's movements in this way? What did you feel when someone else was following your movements?

Notes

If feelings were colours

⑤
🕐 10 mins
♱ ♱ ♱
🗨

☑ empathy
☑ self-awareness
☑ imagination

☑ non-verbal
   communication
☑ observation

How to play   The game coordinator leads a very brief discussion about how different feelings could be thought of as different colours. For example, 'I'm the colour blue today because I feel calm'; 'I'm the colour blue today because I feel sad'; 'I'm the colour red because I feel full of energy'. Ask everyone what colour they would be today and why they would be that colour. Players then try to feel what it is like to move around the room as this colour.

Adaptations   Everyone tries the same colour. Do the movements first and then ask what emotion/feeling players had when they moved as this colour.

Try three or four different colours in succession.

Groups of players choose a colour to portray to the rest of the group who have to guess which colour it is.

Reflection   Do all the blues move in the same way? How do different colours move? Is it easy to change from one 'mood' to another? When might that happen? What colour is anger? Does anger have different colours according to the intensity of the feeling? Did players choose different colours for the same emotion?

Notes

If he/she were a flower

⑩
🕐 10 mins
† †
👄👄

☑ empathy
☑ understanding
  metaphors
☑ concentration

☑ listening

This game works best when the group members already know a little about each other.

How to play Players sit in a circle. Player One leaves the room and the others choose someone in the group who will be described. Player One returns to the room and is allowed to ask ten questions in order to find out who the group have chosen. Each question must take the form of 'If this person were a _____ (flower, house, car, bird etc.) what kind of _____ would they be?' When Player One guesses correctly, another person leaves the room and the process is repeated.

Adaptation Instead of choosing a person, the group chooses an emotion for Player One to guess.

Reflection We all have many different aspects to our personality. Sometimes the way that other people see us is different to how we see ourselves.

Notes

Blind walk

⑧	☑ empathy	☑ supporting
15 mins	☑ trust	☑ giving instructions
	☑ cooperation	
	☑ listening	

This game requires plenty of space for players to move around in. A few large obstacles can be used for players to negotiate.

How to play Divide the group into two. One half of the group will act as silent 'protectors' while the other half of the group is led on a blind walk. The protectors will gently prevent the 'explorers' from walking into obstacles or each other (e.g. by touching them on the arm if they get too close). The explorers choose one leader whom they trust to lead them around the room in a snake formation (with the leader as the head of the snake). Each explorer puts one hand on the shoulder of the person in front of them. The game coordinator, the protectors and the line leader all keep their eyes open. The leader can give verbal instructions. Everyone else in the snake has their eyes shut.

Adaptations Mark out three sides of a large enclosure on the floor. A shepherd tries to round up a group of blindfolded players (sheep) and move them into the pen one at a time using only four words – forwards, backwards, left, right – and a whistle to indicate the number of steps to take.

Players work in pairs and help their partner to 'explore' their surroundings through touch. They can progress from holding their partner's arm to touching an elbow, to just touching finger tips.

Reflection What did you discover? What helped you to feel safe? Was it the reassurance of the leader? Precise directions? Tone of voice? Did you feel able to ask the leader to slow down if needed? What did it feel like to be the leader? Were you aware of how the rest of the snake was coping with the blind walk? Do you think you gave clear instructions?

Notes

Additional notes: more ideas for exploring feelings and developing empathy

Reflections

13

You and me together: building cooperation and negotiation skills

Cartoons

⑩
🕐 45 mins
🛉 🛉 🛉
💬💬💬

☑ cooperation
☑ making judgements
☑ negotiation

☑ understanding
stereotypes

How to play   Players divide into small groups. Each group collaborates to make a cartoon or a collage of a scene depicting an interaction where something has gone wrong or there is at least one person who is feeling 'left out' or anxious. Groups then share their cartoons and try to guess what each other's pictures represent.

Adaptation   Players divide into small groups and devise a one minute silent play, depicting a situation that needs to be resolved. They then act out their plays for the rest of the group to guess the situation.

Reflection   Talk about differing viewpoints and different interpretations of the pictures and plays. Was there any indication of bias or stereotyping? How are these relevant to the ability to cooperate and negotiate?

Notes

Waves on the sea parachute game

⑤

🕐 10 mins

🚶 🚶 🚶

💬

☑ cooperation
☑ listening
☑ concentration
☑ self-control

☑ imagination

How to play   Players stand in a circle, holding the parachute with both hands at waist level. A large soft ball is placed in the middle of the parachute. The game coordinator gives instructions for how calm or stormy the waves on the 'sea' should be and players move the parachute accordingly, while trying to stop the soft ball from falling off.

Finish with a calm rippling of the parachute and gently lay it on the ground. Everyone sits quietly around the outside of the 'sea'.

Adaptations   Tell the story of a storm brewing, from gentle rain to a tornado and then subsiding again. Players move the parachute according to the different stages of the storm.

Have several soft balls on the parachute at the same time.

Players take turns to give instructions for moving the parachute in different ways at ground level (e.g. like ripples on a pond, like great waves, like a sheet of ice) while two or more players walk across the surface in an appropriate way to match the motion.

Reflection   How easy or difficult was it to cooperate to keep the soft ball on the parachute? What happens if one or two people in a group are 'making waves' when everyone else is being calm?

Notes

Splodge tag

⑤   ☑ cooperation   ☑ self-control
🕐 10 mins   ☑ coordination
🚶 🚶 🚶   ☑ awareness of
💬   others

How to play   The game starts in the same way as a normal tag game. The first player to be the 'tagger' runs after the rest of the group. When he or she manages to tag another player they join hands. These two players then try to tag a third and then a fourth player who also join up with them. As soon as there is a group of four players together, they split into two sets and each set goes off to tag two more players and so on until there is only one person left who has not yet been tagged. If the game is to continue this player starts off as the new tagger.

Adaptation   The 'splodge' does not split but just keeps growing bigger and bigger until all the players are part of one big splodge.

Reflection   This game only works well if players cooperate fully with each other. Was it difficult or easy for small groups to cooperate? How did you decide in which direction to run? Were you all trying to run at the same pace? What were the small splodges trying to do? Was it important to stay together or to catch someone else?

Notes

Drawing together

⑦
🕐 15 mins
♀ ♂ ♀
💬

☑ cooperation
☑ concentration
☑ sharing
☑ imagination

☑ observation

How to play   Set out large sheets of paper on tables so that groups of players can move around their table easily. Each group draws a collaborative picture or just makes 'marks' on the paper, using a variety of pencils, pastels and pens. The group coordinator can provide a theme or leave everyone to draw whatever they like.

Adaptation   Draw pictures in pairs. Divide a piece of paper in two so that pairs can draw at the same time or take turns.

Reflection   How do we maintain group cooperation?

What does it feel like to draw a joint picture? How did you feel when someone drew their image very close to yours or changed your image in some way? What was the difference between all drawing different things on the same piece of paper and all drawing a truly collaborative picture?

Notes

Musical balance

⑦
🕐 5 mins
👤 👤 👤
💬

☑ cooperation
☑ trust
☑ self-awareness

This game needs at least 12 people in the circle for it to work successfully.

How to play   Players form a circle with each person holding on to the waist of the person in front of them. They walk around while music is playing. When the music stops they have to sit down gently on the lap of the person behind them. The circle usually collapses the first few times but most groups can eventually manage this very successfully.

Adaptations   Play musical chairs but instead of players being 'out' when chairs are removed, they can balance on another person's lap so there will be more and more people sitting on each chair and they will have to balance carefully.

In pairs, players sit back to back on the floor with their knees bent. They then link arms and try to stand up together.

Reflection   It's OK to make mistakes or for things to not quite work out. By persevering and altering the way we approach the task or by improving our skills we can often solve the problem. Does this game involve a problem or a challenge?

Notes

Vocal orchestra

⑥

⏱ 10 mins

☝ ☝ ☝

♀

☑ cooperation
☑ negotiation
☑ non-verbal communication

☑ concentration
☑ observation

How to play | The game coordinator demonstrates how to 'conduct' an orchestra with hand movements that indicate e.g. loudly/softly, quickly/slowly, all join in, stop.

Each person chooses a vocalization (see *Guess the voice*, p.110). Players stand in a row, in small groups or in a circle according to the size of the group. Conductors take turns to conduct the orchestra as a whole group and with duos, solos etc.

Adaptations | Use movements instead of sounds e.g. hop, jump, stretch, wave.

⑤ | Divide the group up into smaller groups of four before starting. The smaller groups stand together and all do the action or make the same sound when the conductor points to them.

Use home-made instruments.

Reflection | What does it feel like to be the conductor? What does it feel like to be part of the orchestra? What are some of the difficulties involved in being a conductor? What does it feel like to do a solo or duo when you are part of an orchestra?

Do all cooperative games need a leader?

Notes

Talking turns

⑨
🕐 10 mins

☑ cooperation
☑ negotiation
☑ taking turns
☑ concentration

☑ anticipation

How to play   In pairs, players put one arm round each other and act as if they were one person. They talk about a given subject, with each person saying one word at a time to make sentences. This means that they have to guess what the other person is aiming to say and it can get quite frustrating and difficult! Topics could include 'Why I like chocolate', 'What I did yesterday', 'My favourite holiday', 'What I learned at school this morning.'

Adaptation   The audience asks questions and the pair have to answer one word at a time.

Reflection   Did pairs manage to cooperate to make sense even if they couldn't guess what their partner was going to say? Sometimes we think we know what other people are thinking. Sometimes we expect others to know what we are thinking!

Notes

Big ball parachute game

⑤
🕐 10 mins
👤 👤 👤
💬

☑ cooperation
☑ concentration
☑ observation

How to play   Players hold the parachute at waist level and send a very large ball around the circle. One half of the players aim to try and keep the ball in the circle while the other half try and send it out.

Adaptation   Send several different sized balls around the circle, either with everyone cooperating to try to keep the balls going in the same direction or with half the group trying to send the balls out of the circle.

Reflection   Talk about cooperating as a large group. What are some of the real life situations where groups of children might need to cooperate? What happens when some members of the group are not cooperating?

Notes

Working parts

⑥

🕐 15 mins

♦ ♦ ♦

⚇

☑ cooperation

☑ negotiation

☑ problem-solving

☑ creative thinking

☑ observation

You may need to brainstorm some ideas for machines with the group before you start the game (e.g. a CD in a CD player, lawn mower, motorbike, computer with mouse, mobile phone).

How to play   Small teams (around five is a good number) think of a machine that has several working parts. Each member of the team takes on the role of a different part in the machine (and an 'operator'). Players can use sounds and actions and have parts working together or at different times.

Each team practises their machine and then demonstrates it for the other teams to guess what it is.

Adaptations   Teams pick a machine from a prepared set of cards.

Teams invent a machine and explain it to the rest of the group.

Reflection   Did all team members take an equal part? Is it possible for teams to be non-competitive? Did teams have a leader or did all members join in with the decision-making?

Notes

Abandon ship!

⑨
🕐 30 mins
🧍 🧍 🧍
💬💬💬

☑ negotiation
☑ compromise
☑ cooperation
☑ creative thinking

☑ problem-solving

How to play   Split into an equal number of small groups or pairs, according to the size of the whole group. Within each group members imagine that they are on a ship that is about to sink. They have a lifeboat but they are only allowed to take ten items with them from the ship. First they think of ten items each. They then have to negotiate with other team members as to what to take as they can only take ten items between them. Groups then join with another group and renegotiate the ten items. Eventually whole group meet and negotiate a final ten items.

Adaptation   The whole group has been shipwrecked. They have two empty plastic bottles to use on the desert island. Small groups or pairs think of as many uses as possible for the two bottles. The whole group then pool their ideas.

Reflection   How did this feel? Is everyone happy with the final decision? Is everyone happy with how the negotiations went? Did everyone get a chance to put their ideas forward? In the final group did a clear leader emerge? How easy or difficult was it to agree on ten items? What are some of the benefits of working in a group to solve problems?

Notes

Where shall we go?

⑨

🕐 30 mins

👤 👤 👤

🗨🗨🗨

☑ negotiation

☑ compromise

☑ cooperation

☑ creative thinking

☑ problem-solving

How to play Split into an equal number of small groups or pairs, according to the size of the whole group. Players imagine that they are a 'holiday' committee. They have been given the task of planning a day out for the whole group. They must take into consideration any special requirements of group members and must negotiate an agreed day out that they think will cater for everyone's likes and dislikes. After 10–15 minutes each committee chooses a spokesperson to present their ideas to the rest of the larger group. Further discussion and negotiation should be encouraged in order to reach an agreement between all players.

Adaptations Committees plan an afternoon of entertainment for someone else, e.g. the residents of a local care home or a group of younger children.

Reflection How did this feel? Is everyone happy with the final decision? Is everyone happy with how the negotiations went? Did everyone get a chance to put their ideas forward? Being an effective negotiator isn't about getting your own way. Sometimes it involves reaching a compromise or helping others to come to an agreement.

Notes

Skill mix

⑦
🕐 15 mins
🕴 🕴 🕴
💬

☑ cooperation
☑ self-awareness
☑ awareness of
   others

☑ concentration
☑ creative thinking

This game needs some preparation beforehand. You will need to find or draw a large picture of an imposing building such as a castle. Paste this onto card and then cut the picture into enough puzzle pieces to provide one piece for each player in the group.

How to play   Players identify a skill that they are currently developing. This can be specifically related to social skills or could be more general. Each person draws something to represent their skill on the back of a puzzle piece. When all players have completed a drawing the group tries to make the puzzle in a given time limit. This can either be done by using the original picture of a building or by shape alone. Tape the pieces together so that either side of the finished puzzle can be displayed.

Adaptations   Use large plastic bricks or bricks drawn on card to build a structure (wall, house, school etc.) with different assets on each brick or different things that players are proud of.

Reflection   Discuss learning 'sets' of skills and building up abilities gradually. Compare this to having a natural ability which can be practised and developed (such as singing). Are there some skills that everyone needs? How might members of the group share their expertise with others?

Notes

Skill swap

⑩
🕐 30 mins
👤 👤
💬💬

☑ cooperation   ☑ sharing
☑ negotiation
☑ problem-solving
☑ asking questions

How to play   The group is divided into two teams. Each team is given a large sheet of paper on which to make a collage or painting to represent a theme such as 'dance' or 'music'. Team A is given all the materials needed for the activity (coloured paper, paint etc.) but no equipment. Team B is given all the equipment (paint brushes, scissors, glue, sticky tape etc.) but no collage materials. The two teams need to negotiate with each other in order to make their collages.

Adaptation   The theme for the collages could represent a conflict situation such as dealing with bullying.

Reflection   What happened during the trading? What worked? What didn't work?

Notes

Additional notes: more ideas for building cooperation and negotiation skills

Reflections

14

Got it! Solving problems in group interactions

Sort us out

⑦

◷ 10 mins

† † †

◯◯

☑ problem-solving
☑ cooperation
☑ memory
☑ categorization

☑ asking questions
☑ observation

How to play   The game coordinator times the group while they arrange themselves in a line according to one or more of the following criteria:

- alphabetically according to the first letter of their first name
- according to house number
- according to age
- according to what time they get up in the morning.

Adaptations   Players choose their own criteria for organizing the group into a line.

Smaller groups of players stand on a PE bench and then try to arrange themselves according to different criteria without stepping off the bench.

The game is played with criteria chosen that do not need any verbal interaction (e.g. height, eye colour or hair colour).

Reflection   Which line took the least time to organize? Why? Which grouping took the longest? Why?

Think about similarities and differences and how we could be members of several different groups. How does it feel to be a member of a particular group of friends? What is it like to be part of more than one group? What are some of the good things about being in different groups? When is it not so helpful to have separate groupings or gangs?

Notes

The rule of the realm

⑦
⏱ 10 mins
♦ ♦ ♦
🗩🗩🗩

☑ problem-solving   ☑ deduction
☑ listening   ☑ observation
☑ cooperation
☑ memory

This game encourages players to work together in order to solve a puzzle about group rules.

How to play   Divide the group into two. Group A leaves the room. Group B makes up a 'talking rule' such as 'every time you speak you must cross your arms' or 'every time you finish speaking you must scratch your head'. The game coordinator checks that everyone in group B remembers to do this by asking each one a simple question such as 'Do you like chocolate?' or 'How old are you?' Group A returns to the room and the coordinator repeats the previous questions or asks similar ones while group A observe. The aim is for group A to guess the rule. The emphasis is on group problem-solving – if one person in group A guesses the correct rule, this means that the whole group have achieved. Older children can therefore be encouraged to confer before they guess the rule.

Adaptations   Allow a maximum of five guesses.

Rules for older and very able children can be quite complex such as 'when the coordinator asks you a question it is the person on your left who answers' or 'you have to use the last word from the question to start your answer'.

All the group stay in the room and the coordinator chooses a place to set up his or her kingdom e.g. 'the moon', the 'playground'. Each person says what they will bring if they are chosen to be part of the new kingdom. The rule that they have to discover either relates to the first letter of their own name or relates to the first letter of the place where the kingdom will be. The coordinator starts by giving a few examples such as '*S*andeep would be welcome in the new kingdom if he brought *s*nakes with him but not if he brought money. *M*iriam would be welcome if she brought *m*oney, but definitely not if she brought *j*ewels.' The coordinator tells group members if they can join the kingdom or not according to what they offer to bring with them. This needs a strict time limit and therefore clues may need to be made more and more obvious to give everyone the chance to guess the 'rule' and join the kingdom. Players should be encouraged to help each other out towards the end of the game in order to ensure that no one is left out.

Reflection   Do all groups need rules? Why/why not? Are some rules more useful than others? What does it feel like to not know a group rule when it seems like everyone else knows it? What should groups do about that?

Notes

Tangled up

⑤   ☑ problem-solving   ☑ observation
🕐 10 mins   ☑ cooperation
♦ ♦ ♦   ☑ creative thinking
♀   ☑ self-awareness

A well-known problem-solving game which children never seem to get tired of playing!

How to play   The whole group joins hands to form a chain. The person at one end begins to weave in and out, leading other members into a 'tangle' without breaking the links. Players can go over/under arms; between legs etc. Two players then try to untangle the group by giving instructions only. They cannot touch the chain at all.

Adaptation   Players stand in a circle then close their eyes and stretch out their hands to find other hands. They then open their eyes and try to untangle themselves without letting go.

Reflection   How did it feel to be in the role of problem-solver?

What were the important things to remember so that the chain did not break and no one got hurt? Have you ever come across problems that seemed too complex to unravel at first? How should we tackle that sort of problem?

Notes

Step up

⑤

⏱ 15 mins

♦ ♦ ♦

◯◯

☑ problem-solving   ☑ creative thinking
☑ cooperation
☑ listening
☑ trust

This game requires a large space and a supply of 'stepping stones' made from paper or card.

How to play Small groups of around six to eight players per group must cross the designated space by using a small number of stepping stones (not enough to get them all the way across the space). No member of the group is allowed to touch the ground or floor. Five or six stones are normally enough for a group of eight.

Adaptation Groups use the stepping stones to 'rescue' a player who is stranded on the
⑧ other side of the space. The stranded player is blindfolded. If he or she comes off a stepping stone and touches any part of the floor the rescue has to start from the beginning again.

Reflection Was there more than one way to solve the problem? How did group members cooperate? How did it feel to be the stranded player? Did you feel safe? What helped you to trust the group?

Notes

Find the leader

⑤
🕐 10 mins
👤 👤 👤
💬

☑ problem-solving
☑ non-verbal communication
☑ concentration

☑ observation

How to play One person (the detective) leaves the room while the others choose a leader. The detective returns and stands in the middle of the circle. Players in the circle have to copy everything the leader does and the detective tries to spot who the leader is.

Adaptation Have two leaders and two detectives. The leaders lead alternate players in the circle.

Reflection How do leaders ensure they have the attention of the players? Does everyone watch the leader or is it sometimes a chain reaction? Talk about leading by example and leading by instruction.

Notes

Finger carry

⑧
🕐 10 mins
♟ ♟ ♟
💬💬

☑ problem-solving
☑ cooperation
☑ tolerating frustration

☑ creative thinking

How to play   Small groups of players (four to six per group) are given a set of small objects of various shapes and weights which they must transport from one side of the room to the other. Each player can only use one finger of one hand and must keep the other hand behind their back. The aim is to move the objects within a set time limit (decided according to the dexterity of the players and the number of objects being used).

Adaptation   If an object is dropped the players must start from the beginning again.

Reflection   What do you feel when you solve a problem either individually or as a group? What skills are involved in problem-solving? Do you feel comfortable asking for help when something is difficult?

Think of a time when you have helped someone else. How did that feel? How did the other person respond? Has anyone ever helped you out when you didn't need or want their help? How does that feel? What could you say in that situation? (For example, 'Thank you for offering to help but I really want to do this for myself'.)

Notes

Story share

⑥
⏱ 10 mins
♀ ♀ ♀
💬💬

☑ problem-solving   ☑ creative thinking
☑ cooperation   ☑ waiting
☑ listening
☑ sequencing

How to play   The first player starts off a story by stating a 'problem' that needs to be solved. The next player continues the story by saying one or two sentences. The third player adds one or two more sentences and so on around the circle. The aim is for the last person in the circle to bring the story to a satisfactory conclusion while still only using two sentences at the most. A new problem is then introduced.

The game continues for as long as all players remain engaged.

Adaptation   The group is given a selection of catchphrases or objects which must be incorporated into the story in a cohesive way. Players may choose these at random or they have to follow a pattern such as 'every third person in the circle picks an object to include in their part of the story'. The game coordinator can challenge unconvincing connections.

Reflection   Was this easy or difficult? Were players helping each other out? If so, how did they do that?

Were there creative solutions to problems?

Does it help to have more than one person solving a problem? Did other players have different solutions that they didn't get the chance to share?

Notes

Additional notes: more ideas for problem-solving in group interactions

Reflections

15

Wind-downs and celebrations

Parachute wind-downs

If you have been using a parachute for some of the games you could try the following wind-downs:

- Invite all the children to lie still under the parachute while game coordinators gently waft it up and down over the top of them.

- Sit around the outside edge of the parachute and pass a smile or a hand squeeze around the circle.

- Invite the children to lie quietly on top of the parachute, listening to some gentle music or a short story.

Relaxation

⑤

⏱ 20 mins

☑ self-calming
☑ listening
☑ self-distraction
☑ body awareness

This type of relaxation works by focusing the mind on different areas of the body and just being aware of what that area feels like. Often if we try to relax, we try too hard! In our efforts to relax we actually set up more tension. By observing what the body is doing there is a natural tendency simply to allow any areas of tension to relax and release.

What to do   The children can be lying down (e.g. on top of a parachute) or seated. Read each part very slowly and calmly with plenty of pauses to allow everyone time to follow your instructions.

Instructions   When you are ready, let your eyes close gently and settle yourself into a comfortable position.

Notice the feel of your body on the floor (in the chair)…now start to notice your feet… Put all your attention on your feet and really notice what they feel like. Maybe they feel warm or cold; perhaps they are numb or itchy…tight or relaxed. Just notice whatever you can feel in your feet…

Now gently move your thoughts from your feet to the lower part of your legs. Let your thoughts leave your feet and just move very easily to your legs. Notice whatever feeling is there just at this moment… There are no right or wrong feelings… Whatever you can feel is OK…

Now move up to your knees…and then the top part of your legs and notice whatever feelings are there… Now start to notice your body, feel what's happening when you breathe gently in and out…start to think about your shoulders…feel any tightness just melt away… Notice all the feelings around your neck and your head…

Let your thoughts go gently to your back…all along the length of your back…feel the relaxation spreading through your body… Thinking about your arms now. Just notice whatever is there…and down the length of your arms into your hands… Notice all your fingers one by one. Whatever is there, just notice it…

Now, instead of thinking of yourself in parts, feel your whole body relax. Just letting go…letting the floor (chair) support you and just relaxing into it… As you breathe in, breathe in relaxation…and feel it spreading through every part of you…breathing in…and out…like waves on a sea shore… Lie quietly for a few moments and enjoy the feeling of being relaxed…

(Allow at least one or two minutes of quietness.)

Keep noticing your body and start to listen to whatever sounds there are around you… Begin to move your hands and feet a little bit… When you feel ready, open your eyes and look around you… Lie or sit quietly for a short while before stretching and having a yawn…

Source: *Helping Children to Build Self-esteem* (Plummer 2007a).

Reflection   Sometimes if we are very anxious or nervous or tense about something it shows in our body. Our muscles become tight. Maybe they begin to ache a little bit. We might feel 'knotted up' inside. This can feel very uncomfortable. It's a really nice feeling to be able to relax your body and it will help you to feel confident and more able to do things that are a bit difficult.

Notes

Emblems of success

⑦
🕐 45 mins
👤 👤 👤
💬

☑ being prepared
☑ understanding
  metaphors
☑ deduction

☑ self-awareness
☑ self-respect

How to play Players each draw the shape of a shield on a large piece of paper. They divide the shield into four sections and draw different symbols or pictures in each section to show successful strategies that they have used in different social situations. Some possible strategies are:

- talking things over with a friend beforehand
- asking for help
- respecting and valuing myself
- respecting and valuing other people
- walking away from conflict situations
- finding a quiet space to 'chill out'.

Display the shields on a table or wall. Players guess the owner of each one.

Adaptations Draw a shield for my hopes for next year or my motto.

Make one large coat of arms for the whole group.

Make a flag instead of a shield.

Reflection Talk about similarities and differences between the shields.

Talk about and celebrate times when players have used strategies successfully.

Notes

Pack your suitcase

⑧
🕐 5 mins
♀ ♀ ♀
💬💬

☑ imagination
☑ dramatic
   awareness

☑ understanding
   metaphors
☑ empathy

How to play Players are invited to imagine that they each have a suitcase or treasure box that they are going to take away with them when they leave the group. They can choose whatever they want to put into it – perhaps a memory of a particular event or of people in the group, a skill they have developed, a new game that they have learned or something important that someone said to them. Ask each person in turn or ask for volunteers to say what they will pack in their suitcase to take away with them.

Adaptation Players sit in a circle. Each person takes an imaginary gift from a treasure chest in the centre of the circle and presents it to the person sitting next to them, saying what the gift is and why they are giving it to that person.

Reflection How will you remind yourself of your achievements? Sometimes we carry heavy suitcases of worries and troubles with us everywhere we go. Try experimenting with carrying *this* suitcase for a while instead!

Notes

Closing circle

⑦
⏲ 5 mins
† † †
💬💬

☑ listening
☑ trust
☑ taking turns
☑ concentration

☑ self-awareness

How to play At the end of each meeting bring everyone back together again in a circle and finish with each person having the chance to say one brief thing before they leave. For example:

I feel…

Today I found out that…

Today I felt…

My name is…and I am…

I have noticed that…

I feel really good about…

Adaptation Play a version of *Feel it, do it* (see p.122) where, instead of saying their name with various emotions, players do a round of 'I'm brilliant at…' or 'I feel really good about…', expressing the appropriate emotion strongly through body language and facial expression for others to reflect back.

Reflection Do you set yourself goals to work towards? What would you most like to achieve by the end of next week? Next month? Next term? How will you know when you've achieved it? How will other people know that you've achieved it?

Notes

Group yell

⑤
🕐 5 mins
👤 👤 👤
💬

☑ listening
☑ cooperation
☑ self-awareness

How to play   Everyone crouches down together in a huddle. The game coordinator begins a low humming sound and the others join in. As the whole group gradually stands up, the noise level gets louder and louder until everyone jumps into the air and yells as loudly as they can.

Adaptations   Everyone crouches down in a circle facing inwards. Everyone hums quietly and then gradually gets louder as they all stand up together and raise their arms above their heads. Then everyone does the reverse – starting with a loud hum and getting quieter and quieter as they sink down to the ground and eventually they lie down with their feet towards the centre of the circle in complete silence.

Use yogurt-pot shakers to make a crescendo of noise by adding on one person at a time, and then stop one person at a time until there is silence.

Each player makes a noise with something that they have with them – bracelets, crayons, coins, keys. Start slowly, build to a crescendo and then stop one at a time.

Reflection   Talk about beginnings and endings. Talk about sharing experiences in groups and how group games can help us to feel energized and full of confidence.

Notes

Winning the Oscars

⑥
🕐 10 mins
👤 👤 👤
💬

☑ self-confidence
☑ giving and
   receiving praise

☑ dramatic
   awareness
☑ trust
☑ imagination

How to play Cover a wooden spoon or an artist's figure with tin foil. Present this to each child in turn at an imaginary 'award ceremony' for whatever he or she would most like to have award for. This could be a past achievement, a future goal or something completely fantastical. Really over-play their achievement. The whole group celebrates each award with plenty of clapping and cheering etc.

Adaptation Players take turns to be a 'national treasure'. The rest of the group take turns to walk up to this person and shake hands or give words of praise or thanks.

Reflection Talk about the importance of noticing and celebrating our real achievements and sometimes giving ourselves a verbal or an actual reward for our hard work. Think of small ways that we can reward ourselves and reward others, e.g. make Dad a cup of tea, clean Jim's bike for him, pat someone on the back, invite friends round for a game of football.

Notes

Pirate's treasure parachute game

⑤   ☑ listening
🕐 10 mins   ☑ cooperation
👤 👤 👤   ☑ empathy
💬   ☑ trust

How to play   Everyone puts one possession in a 'treasure' box. Put the box under the parachute. Players hold the parachute at waist level and make 'waves'. Divers take turns to go under the waves to gather one piece of treasure and return it to its owner.

Adaptation   Retrieve treasure according to different qualities or shape, e.g. find something wooden, find something made of metal, find something round.

Reflection   Our talents, abilities, personality characteristics and ideas are all examples of our personal 'treasure'. Do you know what is in your treasure box? Make a list of things that you would like other people to know about you.

Notes

Additional notes: more ideas for wind-downs and celebrations

Reflections

Suggested stories
for exploring social skills

Imagination

And to Think That I Saw It on Mulberry Street by Dr Seuss (Harper Collins, 1992).
This is a little boy's tale of his journey from school to home. He wants to tell his Dad what he has seen but he thinks that the horse and wagon that he spotted is far too boring to report. By the time he gets home this simple sight has grown into the most amazing tale imaginable!

The Afterdark Princess by Annie Dalton (Mammoth Books, 2001).
Joe Quail is an anxious boy who is easily worried by things. When Alice comes to babysit she gives him moonglasses and shows him the Kingdom of the Afterdark. Joe finds the hero in himself when he is called upon to save the last Princess of the Afterdark. Also in this series are *The Dream Snatcher* and *The Midnight Museum*.

Self-awareness and awareness of others

For the younger age group I use *Something Else* by Kathryn Cave and Chris Riddell (Picture Puffins, 1995). This is a story about Something Else who tries to be like others but just isn't!

Susan Laughs by Jeanne Willis and Tony Ross (Red Fox, 2001) challenges possible preconceptions about disability (winner of the 2000 NASEN Special Educational Needs Book Awards).

Daisy-Head Mayzie by Dr Seuss (HarperCollins Children's Books, 1996) tells of a girl who suddenly grows a daisy from the top of her head and the various reactions of the people around her to this strange 'difference'. The daisy finally disappears, but the closing pages of the book hint at its occasional return (although it seems that Mayzie is becoming accustomed to it!).

Bill's New Frock by Anne Fine (Mammoth Books, 1999) explores the differences between girls and boys. A funny and thought-provoking book for all ages, this can lead to excellent discussions with children about expectations, rules and children's views on how adults treat girls and boys.

I also like Nick Butterworth's *The Whisperer* (HarperCollins Children's Books, 2005) – a book for young children about prejudice and diversity.

Older children might enjoy *Krindlekrax* by Philip Ridley (Puffin Books, 2001). This is about a small boy called Ruskin who has 'knock knees', a squeaky voice and wears glasses. Will he get the part of 'hero' in the school play? The mysterious Krindlekrax gives Ruskin the opportunity to prove himself!

Kiss the Dust by Elizabeth Laird (Egmont Books Ltd, 2001). Tara is a refugee from Iraq who is trying to adjust to a completely different life in England.

Friendships and bullying/teasing

For younger children I have used the following:

The Selfish Crocodile by Faustin Charles and Michael Terry (Bloomsbury Children's Books, 1999). This is the story of a crocodile that refuses to share the river with any other animals. He develops toothache but no animal will help him because they are too scared. A mouse dares to enter the crocodile's mouth, and all is resolved in the end.

The Brave Little Grork by Kathryn Cave (Hodder Children's Books, 2002) is a lovely story for the younger age group. Illustrated by Nick Maland, this is a story about the value of friendship and overcoming childhood worries.

I Feel Bullied by Jen Green and Mike Gordon (one of the 'Your Feelings' series, Hodder Wayland, 2001). This contains notes for parents and teachers.

Horton Hatches the Egg by Dr Seuss (HarperCollins Children's Books, 1998). Horton is an elephant with a mission – to hatch the egg that a lazy bird has abandoned. He perseveres through all sorts of trials, including being teased by his friends, but he is triumphant in the end.

Older children enjoy:

Friends and Brothers by Dick King-Smith (Mammoth Books, 2001). A lengthier book, but worth lending out or reading a chapter at a time as part of your planned session.

Skellig by David Almond (Yearling Books, 2000). This amazing story won the Carnegie Medal and Whitbread Children's Book of the Year. It is widely used as a year 7 text but is also suitable for slightly younger children. David's little sister is very ill and he feels helpless. Then he finds a strange creature in the garage and he and his friend Mina, carry it into the light. A book about forming close friendships and about support in stressful times.

The Angel of Nitshill Road by Anne Fine (Egmont Books Ltd, 2002) deals with issues of friendship and bullying in a very positive way.

Confidence

There are plenty of children's books about confidence and feeling OK about yourself. These are some that I have used:

Scaredy Cat by Anne Fine (Mammoth Books, 1998). Poppy is afraid of ghosts and monsters but needs to find a way of showing her classmates that she is not a 'scaredy-cat'.

Only a Show by Anne Fine (Puffin Books, 1998). Anna is worried about doing a five-minute show for her class. She is worried that she isn't confident, clever or funny and that she can't do anything 'special'. In the end, her show is a triumph.

Fergus the Forgetful by Margaret Ryan and Wendy Smith (Collins, 1995). Fergus can never remember things like taking his PE kit or his homework to school, but he is a mine of information about 'important' things and manages to help his school win a quiz.

Solving problems

The Lighthouse Keeper's Lunch by Ronda and David Armitage (Scholastic Children's Books, 1994) – a tale about how to foil hungry seagulls so that the lighthouse keeper gets his lunch.

For older children *Hiding Out* by Elizabeth Laird (Barn Owl Books, 2006) is an excellent book about endurance and problem-solving. Peter and his family are on their way home from a holiday in France. His parents have an argument and in the confusion Peter gets left behind. He has no food or money but he finds a cave and the survival games that he had imagined become real.

Subject Index

Author Index

Acknowledgements

The idea for this book was conceived by Stephen Jones, commissioning editor at Jessica Kingsley Publishers.

The front cover illustration was inspired by three friends from a primary school in Cambridgeshire. Thanks go to them and to their parents for permission to use this illustration.

In researching appropriate games for this collection, I have found books by Mildred Masheder (*Let's Play Together*), Donna Brandes and Howard Phillips (*Gamesters' Handbook*), Arnold Arnold (*The World Book of Games*) and Marian Liebmann (*Art Therapy for Groups*) to be particularly useful. For the majority of the games however I am unable to acknowledge original sources as they have been passed on to me by colleagues or have been adapted from familiar party games. Thanks must therefore go to the many game-players who have been kind enough to share their favourites with me over the years and who so enthusiastically keep the tradition of children's games alive in all its diversity.